''When I was a Child

This Book is Dedicated to all Entrants in the Age Concern Competitions, and to their Families.

Front cover illustration from "Margaretting 1912" by Miss G.M. Baker

"When I Was a Child..."

Edited by
June Jones
Julia Thorogood

Sarsen

*Sarsen Publishing,
42 High Street,
Ingatestone,
Essex.*

ISBN 0-9510856-0-3

Printed in Great Britain by Galliard (Printers) Ltd., Great Yarmouth, Norfolk.

Contents

Editors' Foreword

Age Concern (Essex) has been running an Annual Essay Competition through its affiliated clubs and societies since 1951. The essays in this volume have been selected from those submitted between 1975–1984.

As Editors, we would not wish to claim that our choice represents 'the Best' from the decade. We were attracted by essays which convey the feelings as well as the facts of childhoods remembered. We also hope that the book tells something of the story of the generation who were children during the Great War, and who were then precipitated into an age of change.

By no means all of the writers chosen were born in Essex. Nevertheless we found that their essays often gave us new insight into the special character of the County, particularly in its relationship with the East End of London. We have been left with great respect and affection for the writers, and with many more essays which we would like to have included.

We must record our gratitude to Mrs Shephard and Miss Kidner of Age Concern, to Carole Pope and to Miles Thistlethwaite.

INTRODUCTION
"All these things have happened . . ."

Our generation has lived through more changes, than any other period in history.

I was born in Tollesbury, a fishing village. In those days all the smacks were under sail. They used to work at spratting and five-fingering (star-fish).

Their catches were used for fertilising the land. The boats came up to the Hard. Waggons and tumbrils would be up and down the street from early morning until dark, and from villages four or five miles distant. It really was a pretty sight. All coal and the stone for road-making came into the village by barge. The barges went away with a stack of hay or straw for the various concerns which used horses - Police, Army, Buses, London delivery vehicles. Sometimes they would bring in a load of manure from London, termed London Muck by the locals.

As my father and uncles were pilots, bringing vessels up to the Hard, I was often taken out with them for a trip. Sometimes I went with them to work, trawling or oyster dredging. It was a glorious sight to see the sun rise over the water. All this has changed, no smacks, no barges and the village has become a dormitory village. Of course the last smacks were motorised, but even these have finished and gone.

When I was a child we had little transport in the village, only the carrier's carts. They left at 9am and got into Colchester at about noon. If you wished to go elsewhere you had to hire a tub cart, or waggonette. Children used to have to go by carrier's cart to hospital to have their tonsils out and come home the same day.

All children went to school in their own village. Some had to walk two miles. Discipline was strict and the cane used frequently. One change nowadays is that children are more healthy, better clothed, and shod, and are really bonny despite behaviour best not mentioned.

The roads were not Macadamed. In the summer gangs used to come with a large boiler full of tar and huge brooms and cover the surface, sprinkling chippings overall. Water had to be drawn from the well. There were four pumps in the village. Some people had to walk half a mile for buckets of water. There was no street lighting in the village in those days; if we wanted light, we had to use a candle lantern. Us kids used to make lanterns with some wire and a Pinks Jam pot. They would stand a fair wind.

In 1905 the light railway opened. This was known as the Crab and Winkle Line. You got your ticket from the guard on the train. This did not bring prosperity to the village as expected. It carried produce and oysters to Kelvedon, the main line station.

During the summer months people used to work in the fields, pea-picking and fruit-picking, starting at about 4 o'clock in the morning. This has mostly disappeared owing to the use of machinery. Many of the younger men left the village in summer to go yachting. They set off at the end of April and returned about October. People called it the village of yachting widows.

Of course there used to be huge Fairs, all steam, and there would be the Village Fete. Most were quite content with this way of life, much happier than people are today.

Beer was two pence old money a pint, milk one penny, cigarettes two pence a packet. You could buy a dozen boxes of matches for one and a half pence, a loaf of bread for two pence, a large string of plaice or whiting for six pence. You had to be 70 years of age before you could draw a pension. It was then 7/6d. What a change! Few lived to reach 70 and if a person came on hard times a concert would be arranged, as there was no Public Assistance in those days. Before the National Insurance was brought in, many people relied on a Friendly Society such as Foresters, Hearts of Oak or Odd Fellows.

The farming practices have changed. Corn used to be cut with binders, which threw the sheaves out. They were stacked and stood in the fields for at least a week, then carted and stacked in the yard. There they remained till about Christmas when there was not much other important work to do. The stack would then be opened up and threshed. This was done by the steam engine and drum. Care had to be taken when storing, as grain is inclined to heat if at all damp.

Supplementary to farming, you had your blacksmiths and wheelwrights in the village. There were harness-makers, and there were boot-makers who made heavy boots for work on the land and seaboots for the fishermen. Haycutters travelled round cutting up the hay-stacks into trusses. They used large knives and presses for this purpose. All root crops were gathered by hand; potatoes, beet, mangolds.

We as kids, on a Sunday afternoon, used to go to the large farms, where the horsemen would take between twelve and twenty horses to drink at the pond- a lovely sight. When they were threshing, we would go to catch mice and rats. Sometimes we would put mice in our pockets and take them to school. If we were caught with them, we had the cane and a lecture. The culmination of all this was the Harvest Festival, when everyone in the village attended, and raised the roof with the lovely, old, familiar hymns.

The shops, as I remember, were places where you received personal attention. You were able to pick what bacon you wanted. All joints were arrayed on the counter. There would be bags of nuts and chicken feed on the floor. Whole cheeses would be on display and chunks of butter. They weighed up while you waited, and patted the butter into shape. There would be broom heads, brushes, dust pans and kettles hanging on the ceiling. The grocer and his assistants were dressed in white frilled aprons and all out to oblige. People would come in and ask for a pennyworth of tea. A flank of bacon cost about fourpence. There would be chairs to sit on while waiting. The butcher would be farmer as well, grazing his own beasts, and out for perfection. No foreign meat, it was unheard of in the village. One man did start, but had to give up.

Very few people had ovens in their homes, so a lot of the food was taken to the bakehouse. We had four bakers in those days. Some folks used Dutch ovens which you hooked on to the bars of the stove. The grocer and the butcher made weekly deliveries, the baker daily. The Post cost one penny for letters, a half penny for postcards.

The mail used to be delivered and collected by a mail cart. This was a high flyer. If people were in the road when it was coming, they quickly jumped to one side. It left the Post

Office at seven in the evening, stopping in Witham and collecting on the way. One night the clock struck seven, but before the Mailman could climb up, the horse had gone with the Mail!

The milkman used to go door to door with a pail, dipping the milk with ladles into the jugs. Another caller was the rag and bone man. We saved all the bones in an old bucket, and he would perhaps give us a copper or two. Later he gave balloons or paper windmills. He eventually disappeared.

At Christmas we used to visit London. Here was quite a difference. In those days it was horse buses, hansom cabs and growlers, great drays and fine horses. Even in those days there were traffic jams. The lamp lighter went round every evening with his pole, lighting the gas lamps. The Muffin man did his round ringing his bell with his tray on his head. Then there was the Electric Tram. There were a few motor cars coming along.

We then had the intervention of the First War after which came great changes. The internal combustion engine took over. Motor buses replaced the horses, taxi cabs the hansoms. The trolley bus was superseding the electric tram. The war brought the aeroplane into full production and it began to be used commercially. After the Germans bombing of London with Zeppelins, both countries tried to develop airships for commercial purposes but failed to make this a success.

The war had increased the use of wireless communication, and people were making their own sets. Nearly every other house had a crystal set made for a few shillings. The cinema was experimenting with talking films, and the cinema pianists were losing their jobs. Unemployment was running high, and the Labour Party was out to win power. There was an increase in the provision of council houses.

Cycling was still very popular, and the motor car gained favour. The leading motor manufacturers were working hard to produce cheap cars, and Ford eventually succeeded. Petrol was tenpence, a shilling or one and twopence a gallon. Working hours were being made shorter, so people were enjoying more leisure. The charabanc now replaced the old horse brake for beanfeasts.

Fascism was beginning to raise its ugly head, and in some of the large towns, riots broke out. Italians marched into Abyssinia. Germans and Italians helped overthrow the government of Spain. Peace was not to reign for long. Hitler was storming about Europe, and eventually marched into Poland. Thus started the Second War, which lasted six years.

After this much progress was made. Road transport again increased at a great rate.

Coloured films were appearing in the cinema. Motor coaches were running to every part of the British Isles. Planes were flying all over the world. A great National Health scheme was worked out by Lord Beveridge. Many diseases had been conquered. The Board of Guardians was abolished and proper homes were being provided for the elderly. The image of the Workhouse and the Poor Law had gone. The school leaving age was raised to sixteen and child welfare stepped up. Unfortunately courtesy and good behaviour have deteriorated, and wages and the cost of living escalated beyond all reason.

We have seen men landing on the moon, something we never could have guessed would happen. Submarines have travelled under the North Pole, and oil has been discovered under the North Sea. But with all these advances, there are signs that some of them are having an ill effect on our wild life. One sad instance is the oiling up of thousands of seabirds. Some of the sprays are affecting our flora and butterflies. And on top of all this we have kidnapping and mass murder.

As the small business man is being pushed out by the huge combines, we are losing our choice of food. Also, there are so many artificial and tinned foods being used, that one wonders how long it will be before people have lost the art of cooking. All this is happening in such a beautiful and wonderful world. There must be hundreds of other things I have missed, but all these have happened in one lifetime, even the passing of the straw boater and the bowler hat.

F.J.G.

Chapter I
"When I was a child . . . "

I was born in 1906 in a little back street in the East End of London within sight of the East India docks. My first recollection is of the celebrations at the coronation of King George V and Queen Mary.

On this great day we were sent off to school, dressed in our best clothes and carrying our Union Jacks for the grand parade in the school playground. There we sang the National Anthem of each of the Commonwealth countries, finishing the morning with "God Save the King". The Headmaster announced a celebration tea for 4.30 that afternoon.

This was one occasion when nobody was late. The goodies and lemonade disappeared at lightning speed, and to crown the day's events, we were each presented with a Coronation mug picturing the King on one side and the Queen on the other. I have seen these mugs since, for sale in antique shops, and they always bring back memories of times which, though hard, were full of good fellowship and great community spirit.

The area was heavily populated, and I

suppose, on a summer evening, one could count up to one hundred children of all ages and sizes playing in the streets. The games we played were of wide variety - 'kick can copper', buttons and another like leap-frog, but called 'Hi Jimmy Kracko'. They all had one thing in common - noise! One sight, I remember could bring complete silence for a time, and this was when a balloon was seen, floating across the sky. We would gaze at it in wonder, amazed that somebody could be carried in that frail-looking bubble.

The buses on the main Dock Road were the old open decks and the trams were horse drawn. They were slow and easy to catch for a free ride if the conductor was 'up-top'. Outside the railway station at Poplar there were a few horse-drawn cabs. They got most of their fares from seamen, returning home or sailing from the docks. A blast from a ship's horn was a significant thing to most of my friends. Their fathers were either on the ship going off or coming in to dock. We would run up the main road on hearing it, to see which way the masts of the ship were moving. If it was coming in, the next run was to the dock gate to ask the policeman on duty the name of the ship. If it was one of 'ours' (Union Castle Line), it was certain that some of the crew were from our street, so away we would run to carry the glad news home.

The Dock Gates were also a gathering place for other events. The Suffragettes held some of their meetings there, also Dockers Union meetings. Every Sunday evening many people would gather there to listen to the Salvation Army Band.

Then came the War in 1914, bringing changes to affect all our lives. It was a period of new excitement for us younger folk, getting leave from school so that we could 'queue' for rations of margarine or potatoes or whatever happened to be available at the local shops. There was the air-raid policemen riding round the streets with a placard on his chest, which read, "TAKE COVER". At first this was the only air-raid warning during daylight, and I'm afraid we were more intent on seeing the 'Gothas' or 'Taubes' than getting under cover. Our behaviour, at times, must have added more grey hairs to mother's head. Most of the men returned home at the end of the War, and there was a party of welcome in every street, with tables down the middle of the road, and all the food we could muster together.

During the next few years some changes took place. Our old oil lamp at home was put away, and we had gas lighting in the house. Another excitement,

"Can I light the gas, Mum?"

"Yes, and mind the mantle."

It was usually a 'Veritas' and cost the terrible amout of three pence halfpenny.

The speed of invention accelerated after the Second World War with jet engines, diesel engines, wider roads, bigger loads. The tempo of ordinary life seems to have increased to uncomfortable levels, and, although there is no doubt that people enjoy many more privileges than in the days when I was a child, one cannot but look back with nostalgic memories to the days when one could really see the surroundings, instead of having it all flashing past in a blur of 'Modern Times'.

E.B.

Having been born within sight and sound of the great North Sea, I close my eyes and go into memory lane of my very early childhood. Our playground was the beach, and we learned the ways of wind and tides. During the low tide we played on the rocks, picking up starfish and crabs which we put into our small buckets. We also tried to catch little shrimps which are not pink in the water, but creamy white. They are very quick and difficult to catch, but the crabs were much easier.

Our favourite game was with the crabs. We took one each onto the sand and watched to see whose reached its way back to the sea first. They always knew which way to go, Nature being so wonderful. We also liked to gather seaweed and take it home to hang somewhere outside. You told the weather by this - good weather it was hard and dry, wet weather wet and soft. Most visitors took some home with them.

The seaside provided us with lots to do. Often we picked up wood for the fire and also coke and coal. After a rough high tide, followed by a calm sunny day, we searched for cornelians and, if we were lucky, amber. You needed the sun at the back of you so these reddish precious stones showed up. We saved our stones during the winter months. When visitors came in the summer time,my brother used to put some in his pocket, and when he saw people looking for them, he'd get in front and say,

"I've found one! Look!"

and folks would ask to see it, and offer him money. Seldom were they found in the summer time, which then seemed months of lovely settled weather.

I.M.G.

I lived in London as a child. Each day street cries could be heard.

"Any old rags, bottles, or bones?" would send us children indoors, begging for rags to exchange for a balloon or a toffee apple. The chimney sweep would cry,

"Sweep your chimneys, ladies!"
He carried his brushes and sack on his back.

Sometimes we would see a man carrying a big basket filled with slices of meat on skewers. He wore a striped apron and a straw hat. There would be cats of all shapes and sizes following him,

"Meat for your pets, ladies!" was his cry.

The fishseller with mackeral and live eels would call,

"Alive, alive oh! New mackeral, come and buy!" and on Sundays, "Shrimps and winkles for tea ladies! Half pint mug piled up high!" There was the coalman,

"Any coals today, ladies?" and the salt man, with huge blocks of salt on his barrow,

"Salt! Big lumps for a penny!"

"Knives to grind!" Along came the scissors and knife sharpener with his grinding wheel. We could watch the "Chairs to mend!" man repairing cane-seated chairs, and our early morning caller was,

"Milko, milko!" The milkman carried a

big can of milk and served folks as they came with their jugs.

Sometimes on a Sunday, the hokey-pokey man would sell small blocks of ice with slices of fruit in them,

"Hokey-pokey, penny a lump!"

I can remember a man with a miniature round-about for small children. A musical box played as he wound a rope to turn it.

"Come and join us!" It cost threepence.

We would all gather round the lavender lady with her basket.

"Won't you buy my sweet lavender, sixteen flowers for a penny!"

Another Sunday caller was the Muffin Man. He carried his tray of muffins on his head, and he shattered the Sunday peace with his noisy bell,

"Muffins! one penny for six!"

We always knew when the postman was near as he'd rat-t-tat in his special way on the door knockers. Not many folks had letter boxes in those days. The lamp lighter came whistling along the street. He carried a long pole to light the lamps. It had a hook on one end to pull a short chain fixed to the lamp. They were gas lit. Sometimes he would try to be clever and light up without getting off his bike, before going to the next lamp. We heard,

"Water cresses, water cresses!" from

the watercress man, and, in the winter, "Hot chestnuts!" Most days there were street singers, eager for pennies to be thrown from the windows. And then there was the barrel organ man, with his monkey to pick up the coins.

N.A.M.

My husband was born in 1896 and has lived all his life, except for five years, in Saffron Walden. Those five years were spent in France and Gallipoli, 1914-1919. His recollections of his childhood in the town are many and varied.

Perhaps the most picturesque memory is of 'Showing The Garlands' on May 1st. The children would spend the previous day in the woods gathering pegils (cowslips), bluebells and cuckoo pints. A wild orchid was something special if placed in the centre, but was not always obtainable. Some garlands were in the form of a cross, or bound to the hoops that the children bowled along on other days. On May 1st they went from house to house showing their hoops and asking for halfpennies. I daresay those who were earliest made the most money.

In these days of the motor car, we have

forgotten how carriages once drove through the streets. But what a joy for small boys to ride on the back axle of a brougham - until jealous friends called out,

"Whip behind, mister, whip behind!" The whip would snake round to catch them, and the ride ended ignominiously.

It was always easy to know when the wealthy were ill - several inches of straw on the road muffled the clop! clop! of the horses. What a ton of straw we would need nowadays to quieten the noise of the cars! Then death in the house was announced by crepe veiling the door knocker, and arm bands and hat bands of crepe worn with the garments of deepest mourning. The poor could not afford these niceties nor the leeches that the middle class used to cure themselves.

A cruel method of augmenting the small incomes of those times was the catching of small birds to be sold in the London markets, linnets, bullfinches and goldfinches particularly. A 'call-bird' on a hinged stick was fastened tightly with bird-lime and positioned between two nets. Moving the stick persuaded the call-bird to whistle, thus encouraging others to join it. A terrible possibility was that by putting a needle through the eye of this bird they could make it whistle more loudly. Moving the bird was known as 'flurrying' it. My husband vividly remembers an old neighbour calling out to his companion,

"Flurry yer bird, Chumpy!" and then the two nets were pulled over the helpless victims. Perhaps some of these birds made miserable Londoners happier with memories of the countryside, but at what a price!

In those days children's games were of their own devising - tying up the knockers of two doors across the street and hiding to watch results, leaving a halfpenny on the pavement tied to an invisible thread and ready to be jerked away as soon as anyone stooped to pick it up. They jumped over each others backs, 'hoisty-shaffer' it was called, and then the endless fun of marbles, conkers, tops and hopscotch...

F.M.

It is the morning of Good Friday in a street in Stepney in East London. The period is between 1919 - 1940. The narrow street is full of women and girls who are skipping with thick heavy ropes which they have borrowed from the local builders and bargees. The ropes are about two and a half inches in circumference, and stretch across the street from kerb to kerb. They are so weighty that at least three people are needed at either end to turn them.

Why do they do it? Has it some long ago religious significance that has been lost in the mists of time? I have never been able to find out, but I can still see those ropes in my mind's eye, and hear the slap of them on the cobblestones, while the girls and women run in, skip a few steps, and run out again. Skipping in the street was a regular pastime among small girls, but only on Good Friday morning did the heavy ropes come out and the adults take part.

I also remember how, on New Year's Eve, as twelve o'clock struck, the men of the family would seize any implement which could produce a noise, and march round the outside of the house, banging the Old Year out and the New Year in. I have never fathomed why this was done though I have wondered whether it has any connection with the custom of 'first footing' which is so popular in the North of England and Scotland.

There were other customs which formed part of everyday life, when I was a child. In Summer, for instance, the pubs always used to run their 'beanos', when all the male customers would set out for a day at the seaside or in Epping Forest. I remember that in the early days they travelled by horse-brake, but the advent of the combustion engine brought the char-a-banc, and later the more comfortable motor-coach.

This event caused great excitement in the street. Crowds would gather while the small barrels and crates of beer, together with the boxes of sandwiches and pies were loaded aboard. No one intended to die of hunger or thirst on this journey! All this provender was normally supplied by the landlord of the pub, while the cost of the trip, and the meals during the day, were paid for by the men who would have been contributing a regular sum to a 'club' throughout the year.

At last the publican would step aboard and tell the musician to strike up. He was usually a trumpeter or accordion player who would play most of the time while they were travelling. The vehicles were open-topped (until the very last years), and at this sign the children would yell at the tops of their voices,

"Throw aht yer mouldies!"

and a shower of halfpennies would come from the coach to be scrambled for in the road. The party would return about half an hour before closing time so that a farewell drink could be drunk on the home ground.

Another custom, almost a ritual in the East End household, was Sunday tea. In the morning a procession of barrow boys would appear pushing barrows, each covered with a white cloth, and laden with a selection of dainties for the Sunday tea table. There would be freshly boiled shrimps, both pink and brown, cockles, winkles and whelks from Leigh-on-Sea, pickled herrings, glistening white celery, scrubbed that morning in ice cold water, and fresh green watercress. Cos lettuce, radishes and cooked beetroot completed the tempting display. The barrow boys would each push to their particular streets, with their cries of

"Fresh shrimps! winkles! watercress!"

and we would carefully make our choice at the door from our own boy. These goodies were put into the cold box until later.

During the afternoon, as darkness fell, we would hear the tinkle of a bell from the street, and would dash out to buy the freshly prepared muffins and crumpets from the tray, covered with its green baize cloth, that the muffin man was carrying on his head. When teatime approached, we covered our table with a starched, white cloth, and set out these purchases, together with piles of bread and the butter which only came out on Sundays. There were newly baked cakes, jam, and the kettle was set to boil for many pots of tea. All we then awaited was the arrival of the friends and relations who were coming to share it with us.

We children had our own traditions with the games we played. As we had no gardens, the street was our playground. We would collect anything colourful or shiny, pieces of broken mirror, coloured glass, bright paper, then, choosing a buttress or alcove in the wall of a building, would make a grotto. Here we would sit beside our handiwork asking passers-by to,

"Remember the grotter!" by dropping a coin in our tin as a reward for our artistic abilities. Sometimes we made as much as twopence which took us to the pictures on Saturday morning. There we were allowed to stand on a form at the back, and were given a bag of sweets too!

Among the girls there was a practice called 'A pin for a pick'. We would beg, borrow, or steal a thick magazine or a book, and would place bright pictures cut from birthday or Christmas cards in between the pages. We would then walk around among our friends calling,

"A pin for a pick and a jolly good pick!" We used to collect quite a quantity of pins, but what we did with them I cannot remember. I expect they just went into the family pincushion.

There were many games played in the street that have vanished now - hopscotch, five stones, knocking down Ginger, tin can, copper man, all victims of the growth of the motor car. The 'beano' nowadays may take the form of a cross-Channel duty-free trip. Writing this article has evoked many a pleasant memory for me, and many a nostalgic one.

R.F.

Chapter II

"Hard times but happy ones . . . "

Long ago, in the far off days of my youth, we used to have 'best clothes', which were only worn on Sundays, High days and holidays.

Sunday was the highlight of the working folk's week. However dirty a man's job was during the week, on Sunday he looked a different person. Gone were the old suits and flat caps. In their place was a fresh shirt, stiff at front and cuffs, with a stiff linen collar. The suit was usually navy serge, the hat a black bowler. The boots how they shone! We had our pride, they must shine, even though the soles leaked water! Overcoats seemed to last for ever. They were made of heavy black Melton cloth, which tended to go green with age.

Men were proud of their wives and children, and saw to it that they did them credit when they went to church. (Most people did in those days.) Costumes and high necked blouses were favoured by the women. The hats were a sight to see! In Summer, they were of straw with either ribbon trimming or a few flowers. The young girls all wore broderie anglaise frocks. Their hats of straw were decked with poppies or roses. Sometimes the hats were made of black lace or chiffon on a wire frame, and held bunches of cherries or forget-me-nots. In Winter their coats were quite colourful and their felt hats often sported a squirrel's pelt or the wings of a bird.

Boys often wore white sailor suits in summer, navy in winter. The bigger boys wore 'Norfolk' suits. Trousers were worn short until a lad left school. If he started work at early age, he usually wore his father's 'cut downs', which sagged in front, and looked most peculiar at the rear.

Little girls were a matter of great pride. Their best frocks were covered by much befrilled white pinafores till it was time for Sunday School. Their hats with ribbons or wreaths of buttercups or daisies were put on to leave just one curl bobbing in front. All the little girls seemed to have curls in those days. If nature did not give them, curl papers did.

That vanished breed, old ladies, often wore black shoulder capes, bonnets to match were trimmed with black sequins and jet black beads. Indoors they might wear tiny lace caps on top of their heads, maybe covering thinning hair.

Christmas was a great occasion. We did not have a turkey dinner, but usually roast beef with its juice dripping onto the batter pudding underneath. And oh, the smell of the

Christmas pudding! Food today seems lacking in both taste and smell.

In those days folks put something in the children's stockings even if something else went to the pawn shop. Women's best clothes, worn then, were mostly blouses and skirts, no sweaters in those days. My Mother used to say,

"Pride feels no pain!"

when she saw young girls refuse to put something over their unseasonable silk blouses. We had big coal fires and they were willing to risk a head cold for their day of glory.

So to Lent, and miserable times, no flowers in the Church, midweek as well as the Sunday Services, and extra Sunday School for the youngsters. On Good Friday we had Hot Cross Buns delivered. They were really hot, full of fruit and spices. Mother went to Church for three hours and came home looking miserable.

Easter Day was a joyful one. The Salvation Army marched the streets with banners flying and the band playing "Up from the grave he arose". The churches were full of flowers, and new clothes to worship in were a must.

We all loved Easter Monday, for on that day Dad took his family out for a walk. Out came the best clothes again. Dad never attained the working man's dream - a 'gold Albert' watch chain to wear across his waistcoat, but maybe his pride in us compensated him.

We always took the same walk up Hogg Lane with its row of old cottages. Past this it was all dusty country lanes rutted by cart wheels, flanked by ditches, and a chalk quarry with its deep pits one side, farmland the other. What a lovely day it was with budding trees, singing birds, and a song in our hearts. Dad had given us a penny each and we knew where to spend it! Over the stile, keeping to the footpath till we reached the kissing gate, which led to the churchyard with its well tended graves, North Stifford church, and the tiny village with the thatched cottages. There it was, the small shop where we bought our sweets and rested on the village green.

We set off home, not by the fields, but past the big house and back to Hogg Lane. Dad met up with lots of his workmates on these walks, all proudly shepherding their families. Men were gallant in those days, and Dad always raised his hat to their women-folk.

Whitsun followed the same pattern, on with the best clothes and out with Dad and Mother. This time we walked along Mensons Lane which was another dusty path with chalk quarries at one side. The woods were full of bluebells, 'shirt buttons', and many other flowers. This path also led to North Stifford and its tiny shop.

On August Bank Holiday, we walked

past Hangman Wood with its fearsome Dene Holes, up the steep gravel path, past fields of cabbages, potatoes, corn until we reached Tyrols Heath. This wood was larger though not so exciting as the other. There was a small fair with roundabouts, also a stall selling lemonade and sweets. Mother had brought a kettle and we made a fire of twigs to enjoy tea and sandwiches. Needless to say all Grays and their children seemed to be there, so there was a lot of chatting done.

At Harvest Festival, my sister and I staggered to the church with a large, decorated loaf. The church looked lovely, fruit and flowers everywhere, and we nearly took the roof off with our hearty singing. Lots of folk were there who didn't normally come. Mother said they came for "loaves and fishes".

The Church Sunday School outing was a day at Southend. The beach was full of London folk. The women wore paper ostrich feathers in their over-large hats. The men seemed to like big black-and-white check caps. Sometimes they wore check trousers. Their boots were yellowish brown. They used to sing and dance to a concertina, the women showing a lot of leg in doing so. Maybe they were more than a little drunk, but they were enjoying a day away from the toil of their everyday lives. They paid for their drinks and never seemed to fall out amongst themselves or hurt others.

We had our tea in a big hall with long tables. It consisted of bread and jam sandwiches, plain grocer's lemon and caraway seed cake. The seed stuck in our tender gums and we did not like it much. We thought longingly of tea at the cockle shops.

We dearly loved going to the Peculiar Peoples Sunday School outing. The little girl next door attended this chapel, and by paying 6d my sisters and I were allowed to go with them. The rules of the chapel were very strict. No member must drink alcohol, smoke, go to music halls, theatres or dances. Even watching the Pierettes in the park was taboo. But, my word, they knew how to make little children happy! Mother made us each a flat cotton bag which was tied with tapes under our frocks. This held our precious pennies and a packet of egg sandwiches. Off we went full of excitement, wearing our white frocks and best straw hats.

The brake was drawn by two hefty horses. In we climbed with instructions to get out when we reached a steep hill. Everyone sang going along. They were not our church hymns, but we sang "Will there be any stars in our crowns?" quite as lustily as the others. What a thrill it was to jog along through the countryside, and we were ready for our sandwiches when we arrived at a big field. We were given mugs of tea and later had scrambles for gooseberries and toffees, then games and races. I managed to fall over, someone tied up my knee and gave me a little doll. In view of the fact that we did not attend the Sunday School they were very kind.

No more outings, no bank holidays till Christmas. A seaside holiday was something one only met up with in books, but we were content. We still had our Sundays with rest from school and work, the table laid with a crochet lace edge cloth, best china, a fruit cake, and,joy of joys, sometimes watercress from Springhead Gardens or Gravesend shrimps. Sunday tea was an occasion.

Were times good? Mother said we children were blessed. I still remember class-mates going to soup kitchens during strikes, and staying away from school for want of shoes. The poor youngsters were given school boots, heavy clomping things which advertised their origin.

As I look out of the window of my little council flat, I hear the sound of children on their way to school. They are all well fed and clothed. Our Welfare state gets some things right. God bless the little chatterboxes! They are our joy in the present and our hope for the future.

P.M.B.

In those days people would line their children's overcoats with brown paper. Put between the coat lining and the coat, it would help to keep them warm. I knew a lady who lived near a textile mill. When the blanket which covered the huge rollers was changed, the old one could be bought for a few coppers. Accordingly she would buy it, dye it, and make her children winter coats. Blakeys were used a lot on shoes and boots. Mine were covered with them. I felt more like a horse, but they stopped wear and tear, and were lovely for striking sparks out of the kerbs. We wore white pinafores for school. They were white cambric or calico, and had frills on the shoulders and round the bottom. My mother would starch them and use 'goffering irons' (rather like the old curling tongs) to crimp the frills. These pinafores saved ones clothes as well as looking pretty.

Then, just before Christmas, a neighbour of ours would bring in a large box of felt hats for little girls. He worked in a warehouse in London and my sister and I would have a hat chosen from his selection. There were red, brown, blue hats all in rustling tissue paper. A real ceremony would be gone through before we were suited. Then bands of artificial cherries were draped round the hats and I used to think that I would burst with excitement and pride. The same thing would happen before Easter, but with cream straw hats and wreaths of artificial daisies and corn flowers.

I remember, as a child, seeing ex-soldiers who were out of work, pushing prams with old-fashioned gramaphones. They would stop and put a slatted board on the pavement, then do a tap dance to the music. Even though I was only nine or ten, I felt that this was very sad. There were the barrel organs which I loved. Men could hire them by the day. One man had a dancing bear. It was on a chain and was muzzled. It shuffled up and down to music played by its owner. It was a big bear. One of our neighbours danced with it. I thought she was terribly brave because its claws could have done a lot of damage.

There were lots of street singers. They mostly sang hymms and seemed to come around on a Sunday afternoon. I suppose that was when everyone was at home in London itself. Sometimes in the suburbs you would see four or five men in a group, singing beautifully and in harmony. I used to wonder whether they were unemployed miners. There was a lot of poverty about — no Social Security!

But, in spite of poor wages and unemployment, people knew how to enjoy themselves. I used to stand at the end of our road and watch the brakes go by. These were horse drawn and quite splendid affairs, black with red scrolls around them. Each brake had its own trumpeter to play all the hit tunes, and on the return journey the brakes were often decorated with flowers and bunches of watercress. Everyone would be singing lustily and were very happy, forgetting their troubles for a day.

A friend of mine who lived in Hackney or Bethnal Green, said that her father always took a linnet in a cage when he went to a public house. When the bird heard the noise and the chatter it would start to sing, but only if covered up under a black cloth. I never saw this happen, but she said that lots of men took their linnets in this way, and would have competitions.

It has fascinated me since I have become old, to remember the lovely games and the seasons for playing them which seemed to come naturally, not tied to specific dates on the calendar. There were iron hoops for the boys, with iron hooks to control them. The girls had wooden hoops with wooden batons to push them along. I believe that the iron hoops were called 'skimmers'. Hoops were an autumn and winter game. Marbles were more of a summer game, as were tops. The girls used lighter tops. They were called 'boxers', so I assume that they were made from boxwood. The boy's were called 'peg tops'. Skipping was an all year round game. Five stones was usually played on the doorstep, and even now seems rather complicated. Most of these games have disappeared because of the congestion on the streets. So old customs pass, yielding place to new.

J.I.

I was born in 1913 and I can't remember much about the First World War. I can remember my Dad coming home on leave. I was about as high as the kitchen table, and a bit scared of this stranger who sat me on his knee.

My Granny used to live at Horndon-on-the-Hill. My mother and I would go on the train to Stanford, then walk up an uphill line past a pump where we always had a drink of water. Granny was the village midwife of sorts. They called her Nurse Clarke. She lived in an Almshouse with several other ladies, who always wanted to invite us into their places. One of these was Mrs Crick. Granny said that she was a witch. She used to put a knife under the mat. Granny said that she would never cross over the step, and she never did. I don't think that Mrs Crick was a witch. I think that these ladies were very lonely and loved to see children.

My mother met my Dad when he was a postman, and she was the parlour maid at a lovely house in New Road called 'The Echoes'. Mum used to go to the Garden fete every year there. There used to be Greek dancing by the girls of the convent, dancing on the lawn, and sideshows. Mrs Seabrooke, the lady of the house, always paid for Mum's tea and mine, and asked her about all the family.

We didn't get bored, like some children today. We had too much to do.I was outside the butchers at 7 o'clock every morning, waiting to get meat for ourselves and several neighbours. We used to hire an old bike for six pence for three hours. I think every kid in our area learned to ride the hard way, as these bikes had no brakes. I wonder we didn't have more accidents. Once my brother had a broken leg and another brother was sent to borrow an old lady's bath chair. He and my sister got it, then spent the afternoon having turns up and down Grays Hall Hill, until they careered into a milk float.

Children used to leave school at fourteen years. I didn't want to leave. We had a lovely teacher called Mrs Burrows. On Mondays we used to take her washing in an old wicker basket to another lady, then fetched it back clean on Thursdays. Mrs Burrows was so kind to us. We used to take our dog, Nelson, with us, and we must have been scruffy, but she always gave us a glass of milk and a piece of fruit cake. Even the dog got a bowl of milk.

We also had to go to the Co-op for the dividend winter and summer. Once I lined up all morning for my Mother's divi and a neighbour's. When I got home, the neighbour said that there was a pound short. My Mum had to give her divi to the lady,but I knew I hadn't lost it. I went back to the Co-op, and said that if they were one pound over at the end of the day, they would know that they had given me short money. The agony of that day! But I was right and we got the money back. Once I lost a half crown down a drain, and my Mum sent me to follow the drain man, and ask him to look for it. They used to scoop up the mud in those days. Anyrate, at the third scoop, there was the half crown, the relief of that!

Girls used to go out to service at the big houses. They worked from six o'clock in the morning, until ten or eleven o'clock at night. Some ladies were kind but others were very strict. My sister-in-law said that she was a qualified cook in two years. She could do everything. The lady showed you once and you had to do it then.

They were hard times but happy ones. I went to work at the Mill. I enjoyed it once I got used to the noise. Children are lucky today. I loved the old Carnegie Library at Grays. It opened a wonderful world to me. I love a good book now.

A.E.D.

We must have looked a scruffy pair of urchins as we stood there arguing. We had been blackberrying and had, in fact, collected enough to fill a fair sized shopping basket, about twelve pounds, I should think.

We had started out early in the morning to cover a distance of some eight miles to the woods at Wormley in Hertfordshire, where we had collected our berries. We had travelled from our home in Waltham Abbey on an old bicycle. And, when I say old, it was no more than the truth. The cycle had no mudguards, no bell and, of far greater importance, it had no brakes. The frame was far too big for me, and it was only with my leg at full stretch, that I could reach a pedal with my toes.

I was very proud of that old bike. In those days, over sixty years ago, when most children had very little in the way of toys, I, a small boy of eleven, had my own, my very own bicycle. It was fitted with steps, a short extension tube screwed on to the back axle. My brother, aged about eight, who was my companion, had done our eight mile journey standing on these steps, steadying himself with his hands on my shoulders.

I was dressed in a dirty old pair of trousers, miles too big for me. They were as usual an old pair of my older brother's. The bottoms were frayed where some six inches had been cut from the legs, the knees and backside of the garment were torn. In those days poor kids wore no underpants, and I was somewhat sore where my bare bottom had been chafing on the saddle as I struggled to reach the pedals. I had a pair of boots which were worn and broken, (I forget whose cast offs they were,) and one of Father's old caps, naturally far too big, and worn in the style that Jackie Coogan made famous.

My brother was probably dressed a little better, mainly, I suppose because there was nobody to hand clothes down to him. By the time I was done with them, even the rag and bone merchant was not keen to have them.

We were arguing because I had pushed out into the road, with the basket of blackberries hanging from the handlebars, and was preparing to mount. My brother, however, had spotted a large notice which read, "DANGER! It is extremely dangerous for cyclists to ride down this hill." Unfortunately the hill was not very apparent at this spot. The road seemed nearly level to me.

"Let's walk," said my brother.

"It'll be all right," I replied. "Jump on. I'll get off before we start going too fast."

I straddled the bike. My brother mounted the steps, and away we went, slowly at first, then quickening as the ground started to drop away. The pace became faster..

"Let's get off," said a nervous voice at my back.

"Just a bit further," I said.

Suddenly we turned a corner, and there yawned the steepest hill I had ever seen. A note of panic from the back,

"Let's get off! Let's get off!"

A near scream from me,

"I can't! I can't! We're going too fast!"

It was a very long hill, and by this time we were literally flying along. The wind whistled past my ears, and I hung on for grim death as the runaway bike bounced and rattled along.

I could see quite clearly that at the bottom of the hill was a brook, spanned by a narrow bridge. Each side of the bridge was a low red brick wall, and blocking the whole space between was a donkey pulling a cart.

My brother, looking over my shoulder, saw the danger, and decided to jump clear. The bike gave a terrific wobble. Somehow I kept my hold on the handlebars, and in the split second before the wind caught my cap, blowing the peak under my chin, completely covering my face, I saw the donkey driver. He had realised what was happening, and was frantically trying to back the donkey off the bridge to give me enough space to flash past. Then I was completely blacked out by the cap.

Conscious only of terrific speed, in pitch darkness, I was petrified as I sped on. I heard shouts, screams, stamping of hooves, grinding of wheels and then a fearful crash. I could feel myself sailing through the air, and then the terrific thud as I hit the ground. I slithered along the gravelly road, and then all was quiet.

As from a great way off, I could hear feet running. A voice shouted,

"He's dead! Look at the blood!"

I slowly opened my eyes and eased myself upright. The cap fell from my face, and I was appalled by the sight of pools of blood. I had hit the cart, fair and square. The impact had caused both the basket of fruit and I to take to the air. I had crashed down on it and skidded along the road on the berries. These gave the impreesion of a long trail of blood.

Gradually I gathered my wits. The donkey driver, getting over his shock, started threatening me. My brother was crying, nursing badly grazed knees, and reminding me that he had said we ought to walk. My much-prized bike was a complete write-off, even the frame was broken. I seemed to be the only one who was pleased that I was not badly hurt.

The donkey driver drove off, mumbling about the damage to his cart, and saying that if I had killed his donkey, he would have killed me. I sat by the roadside contemplating my ruined treasure, hopelessly trying to fit the broken parts back together. It was my brother who brought me back to reality by reminding me that the smashed wicker basket might prove to be more serious. How prophetic his words turned out to be.

We wearily tramped the eight miles home, related what had happened, and promptly got a hiding from my stepmother. We were sent to bed without any food for being so careless as to smash the basket and lose all the fruit. I was stiff and sore for days but didn't dare tell anyone, in case it brought forth more punishment to teach me not to be so stupid again.

G.F.S.

Chapter III

"Oh what delightful memories . . . "

Oh, what delightful memories arise when I think of Mother's Baking Day. Even now the smell of baking makes the memories come flooding back.

How good it was to run home from school, on a cold crisp day, and burst into a warm bright kitchen, full of delicious goodies which we knew we would soon be eating! I can recollect, when I was small (my nose could hardly touch the table) gazing in wonder as Mother, with deft hands turned a lump of dough into such a smooth sheet of pastry, and then again transformed it into mouth-watering pies and gorgeous jam tarts.

Although we did possess a Gas Cooker, Mother always preferred to bake in an open fire 'Kitchener' oven.I remember it well, the ash pan was covered by a 'tidy' which had a cast of Lord Kitchener at the front of it. The stove was black, and must have been hard work for Mother to keep so shiny. The oven had no temperature gauges, yet Mother always seemed to know when it was just right.

Sometimes there was a bread pudding ready for our tea. It was dark and spicey and filled with fruit. We could smell it baking even from the street door. And the day she baked bread never failed to bring delight. We would see the bowls of dough arranged across the hearth to help with the rising. Then we knew that later in the day there would be warm, fresh bread.

When Birthdays or Christmas came around, we were allowed to help clean the fruit, (no packets of cleaned dried fruit in those days). We also helped helped grating almonds, and making bread crumbs. Our greatest delight was when we had to stone raisins. Mother would spread a clean cloth on the table, and we were each given some raisins and a small bowl of water for sticky fingers. If it was for a Christmas Cake, and Father was around, he would tell us to sing carols, warning Mother to listen if one of us stopped singing, for then she would know that we had popped a raisin into a willing mouth.

Mother had no scales to measure the ingredients, everything was weighed by table-spoon or cup. As a child this was magic to me. Sometimes, as a treat, my sister and I were allowed to scrape out jamjars, treacle tins, or any other utensil we could find. My sister loved to scrape the bowl. Fortunately that never appealed to me, so she was more than content.

We were also allowed to stand on a chair, and pummel, shape and pound any pieces of pastry left over. All this gave us, I am sure, a feeling of warm security at home, and it is a feeling that I have tried to convey to my own children.

Memories such as these are surely needed by the aged, in this cold hard world of today.

R.D.

I could not resist the offer to write about Market Day. Market Day was one of the greatest joys of mylife when I was a child, living then quite near Queen's Road, Upton Park. I can still remember the excitement I felt when I knew my Mother would be taking us, especially at Christmas.

Unless you have yourself experienced this delight, you cannot begin to know the happiness that it brought us. I can remember my sister and I holding Mother's hand, trying to suppress our excitement, knowing full well that she was setting out to buy all those little extras that would make our Christmas.

Markets in those days, were not restricted at closing time, so we usually left it until it was quite dark, since most of the bargains were to be obtained then. The stall holders would rather sell their wares off cheaply than take them home.

As we walked through the dimly lit streets, we could see the glow of the market before us, and hear too, the cries of many vendors. When at last we arrived, it was like stepping into Fairyland. Each stall was lit by a huge Paraffin Lamp that hissed and flickered alternately.

The Christmas Cracker stall was usually the first stop. We gazed with admiration at the huge crakers on the top of the stall and wondered how many children would be needed to pull them. The stallholder's patter was always amusing. He coaxed and tried to persuade the crowd that it would be heartless to let the kids be without crackers,

"Now Missus," he would say to no-one in particular, "Would you give me a quid for this box?" Without waiting for an answer he would continue,

"Well I'm not asking for a quid...not even for ten bob, 'ere you are, just for a few customers as I like the look of...five bob, and that's me last offer."

We would look at Mother, speechlessly urging her not to refuse such generosity.

Then there was the toy stall that no child could ever pass by. Dolls dressed in glorious clothes, baby dolls, toy prams, tea-sets that were almost as big as Mother's, and so very many other toys which we loved, and which are now gone forever. The nearer we got to Christmas, the better the bargains seemed to be. A man would fill Mother's bag with oranges,

"Only a tanner, little 'uns, just right for the kids."

The market also had its delights in summer time. We were tempted by the Hokey-Pokey man,

"Come on kids, penny a lump, the more you eat, the more you jump!"

There was also the Sarsparella man with his barrel of sarsparella.

It was served cold in Summer, warm in Winter, and was the nicest drink that anyone could wish for!

At the china stall, we would stand, horrified, watching the men juggling with cups and saucers, throwing them up in the air, catching them again on a tray.

There were times too, when the crowd could only struggle to pass by, for Jack-the-Lino-King was in operation, pulling out his rolls right across the road, selling his remnants at ridiculously low prices.

To attract the crowd at the household linen stall, the vendor threw every child a new handkerchief, saying wryly

"I don't want any dirty noses round my stall!"

Then there was always the beautiful

weighing machine with its brass shining, and that little chair swinging ready for you to sit on. If its owner wasn't doing much of a trade, he would pick people out of the crowd, and guess their weight. If he was wrong, they did not have to pay, but I myself, never knew him to be wrong.

Frequently there was a man, sometimes a woman, fortune teller standing in a corner. I suppose it must have been illegal as I often saw them pick up their bags and disappear like a shot.

On a Wednesday morning there was a Pet Stall. There were puppies, kittens and rabbits and, best of all, the chickens. Occasionally the stall holder would raffle some of the chickens. I can remember that Mother returned home, on at least three occasions, with a Buff Orpington laying hen which had only cost her threepence, and supplied us with brown eggs each day for breakfast.

Alas! Queens Road, still a market, has lost all its delights for me now. People in these affluent times lack the zest and happiness to shop, which we experienced. I hope and pray the day will come when I can say to my grandchildren, "Ah! Now THIS is what I call a market!".

R.D.

Saturdays were always welcomed by my little sister and I. Although we walked the same stretch of road to school and home, twice daily, Mondays to Fridays, on Saturdays we were free to meander by the roadside puddles, or to scramble to the tops of frequent granite-stone heaps which awaited a roadman's shovelling, then the slow-motion crunching of a large steam roller.

We were promoted to do the weekly shopping in 1920. Father worked on the farm for six days weekly from dawn to dusk. Mother and he had been quite overwhelmed by the sudden death of their only son, Reggie, at the age of 14 years. As my brother was two and a half years older than I, he had previously been entrusted by my mother to do the usual Saturday shopping in the next village's General Store.

Before we left home on our new venture, Mother insisted upon going through the list which she had prepared. She then advised upon pork and bacon cuts which I must not accept, "wet or dry",

Then, mid-mornings, my sister and I were each given a large boiled sweet, the carpet bag, and the purse, filled with farthings, ha'-pennies, pennies, silver threepenny bits, six-pences, was placed deeply into the base of the bag.

As we walked along we sang a favourite ditty of ours,

"Half a pound of tuppenny-rice,
Half a pound of treacle,
That's the way the money goes -
Pop goes the Weasel!"

Occasionally a stoat or a weasel did dart across our path. We never solved why the weasel had to 'pop', but the little song kept us happy as we walked.

After our journey to the shop, we were pleased to open the lower-half door and set in motion the clanging bell. If we failed to close the door at once, then the elderly Misses Goodsome, were quick to remind us that they were very busy and that little girls were to be seen but not heard in their shop. If others were ahead of us, we awaited our turn sitting upon hessian sacks (1'2 cwt) filled with products from the local mill. They contained barley-meal, 'dan', tail-wheat, maize or household flour.

Hanging over-head were huge creamy coloured bladders, filled with pure white lard. Hefty legs of fresh pork hung from other large steel hooks, an entire pig's 'pluck', trotters and 'lights'. On the chopping board, were up-turned basins of brawn and dripping.

Old Benjamin was in charge of the slaughter house at the rear of the shop, and if he lingered, whilst bringing in further meat supplies to satisfy a customer's needs, Martha, the elder spinster-owner, reminded him, scathingly, that her shop would close at eight o'clock that evening, and that then, only then, would he receive his weeks pay from her hands.

The high mahogany counter bore three sets of scales. The small gleaming brass chain and dish balance was used to weigh powders, pepper, ground-ginger, Epsom Salts or bi-carbonate of soda, small sweets such as raspberry drops or extra strong white pepper-mints. The large flat-veined, marble plates. linked to the main stand

larger amounts of sugar, rice, oatmeal, flour, soda, fats. At the distant end stood the huge scoop holder and the heavier iron weights, marked in pounds and stones.

When, at last, my sister and I stood by the counter to receive the Misses Goodsomes attentions, I had to name the items and quantities which Mother wished to purchase. Brown treacle was always listed, for it was cheaper than Lyle's Golden Syrup, with its printed Old Testament story of "Samson and the Beast". During hot weather the treacle was quickly run from the keg into the jar beneath. Filling the pot was much slower in cold weather, and tying the greaseproof paper over the top of each pot, would prove to be a tricky task. The Misses Goodsome gave vent to their mood in staccato "Hum"s and "Ha"s, warning us to,

"Be sure and keep it upright all the way home."

Finally after checking the goods and paying for them, I handed my mother's shopping list for Miss Goodsomes's signature and thanks. We shared the weight of the carpet-bag, gripping a handle each as we walked side-by-side on our homeward journey.

Mother always brightened herself when we returned and called us "her good girls", and praised us for running that errand, now that Reggie had gone to be an Angel.

Usually Mother approved all our purchases, but whenever she had stated, "a piece of streaky salted pork", which had been extracted from the brine pot at the shop, and therefore served dripping wet, I was reproached for bringing home an inferior cut. Despite my truthful plea that I'd requested (very quietly), NOT the belly part, Mother held aloft the despised portion saying,

"When you can see a pig's teats studded on the rind you must refuse it there and then, for when it's cooked and ready to eat, those teats will still be there, and I can't abide seeing them. Remember! a sow has eight pairs of teats for often she produces sixteen piglets in one litter, and her babies all suck together with no set meal-times."

Needless to add, that in future shopping trips, I learned to be vigilant when buying mother's groceries, and,

"Never spend a penny where a half-penny will do."

I still find shopping a pleasure, even in these hectic days. Only last week I saw a young Mum in the local super-market, with her little daughter perched on her steel shopping trolley. As she loaded her 'pusher', the child commenced singing "Pop goes the Weasel". I doubt whether she knew the delights of boiled rice and treacle, as we frequently enjoyed for our mid-day meals in 1920.

H.D.

I must have been about six years old when I paid my first visit to the cinema, accompanied by my parents who were avid cinema-goers. The cinema seemed a huge building to me. It was situated in the Barking Road, East Ham, and I have an idea that it was called the Empire, though to its patrons, it was the 'Penny Pictures.'

The man at the door was dressed in a most resplendent uniform. He sported rows of gilt buttons, an elaborate peaked cap, and a huge drooping moustache. He had the job of marshalling the queues towards the box office.

Inside there were rows and rows of

long forms with no arm pieces. The usherettes would urge more and more persons to,

"Pass along there, please." in order to accommodate more viewers. It was quite common to have secured a good vantage point whereby one could peer between the heads of those in front, only to move along, please, and find oneself behind a large hat, very seldom removed.

There was a rumour that free cups of tea were served to patrons. At times we heard the sound of cups rattling in various parts of the auditorium, but were never fortunate enough to receive one.

The films were given special emphases by the pianist, who played throughout the programme, slow music for sorrowful scenes, lively tunes, full of vibration when the film reached an exciting moment.

The films most vivid in my memory were those in serials, 'The Perils of Pauline',and others, starring those brave heroines, Pearl White and Ruth Roland. They were always being pursued and captured by villians, huge, swarthy men with enormous black moustaches wearing large sombreros. The heroines were constantly being tied to railway tracks. Then a train, belching out great clouds of black steam would come rushing towards the fair victim. The pianist strenuously worked towards a climax. Nearer and nearer came the train, then lo and behold! the scene changed, and there was the hero, tall, strong and fair, galloping to the rescue. Would he reach the maiden in time? A flashback to our heroine, extreme terror on her face, the train still thundering towards her...THEN, on the screen, TO BE CONTINUED NEXT WEEK, and we dropped back on our forms exhausted.

The serial was usually followed by the Pathe News, featuring presentations, a march past, or a glimpse of eminent foreign visitors. The big film followed.

It would have starred either Charlie Chaplin or Mary Pickford. What a pretty girl was Mary Pickford, petulant at times, endearing, always getting into scrapes, but oh those lovely fair curls! How I envied her! I had only my straight dark hair. Mother would 'do me up' at night with what were commonly called 'rags'. I held one end of the narrow piece, while she twisted my hair round the other half. Then she brought my piece over, twisted that round her section and tied it at the bottom. In the morning, the rag was removed, and the hair brushed round a certain small rod. And there I was - not a bit like Mary Pickford!

Charlie Chaplin was always getting into scrapes. One felt sorry for him, such a down-trodden, pathetic little figure, though most of his troubles were brought about by himself.

As in the serials, the villain was always portrayed by a huge, dark, person, with heavy, beetle brows.

I well remember in the days of the silent films, the plots were made easier to understand by descriptions or remarks appearing on the screen. I often think of my mother sitting with Dad on one side and me the other. When these words appeared, Mother, who had perfect sight, was first nudged by Dad,

"What's that say?" and then by me,

"What's it say, Mum?" Most times she would exclaim in desperation,

"Now I've lost it!"

The usherette used to parade along the gangways holding aloft an object which sent out periodically such a lovely spray of perfume. If I were near enough, I would hold out my hankie, hoping that some would fall on it.

The time would come for us to depart, and we would make our way out of the auditorium, the floor of which was strewn with orange peel, peanut shell, paper bags and more. What a job it must have been for the women to clear up afterwards! Most of the Picture-Houses were known as 'Flea-pits', and I well remember my poor old Mum, when she reached home saying,

"I know I've got one on me!"

H.H.

Chapter IV

"I knew what heaven was all about . . ."

In my elder brother's cut down trousers, a jacket borrowed from a friend, and the whitest shirt in North London, I was done up a treat, and about to embark on the greatest adventure of my life. I was nine years old and, for the first time, I was going to the sea. As a boy in Tottenham during World War I, I knew all about the horrors of the war, but I also knew what heaven was. Heaven was Southend on a Summer's day. I had dreamed about it for weeks.

The charabanc pulled up at the end of our street. Mothers and Fathers, Aunties and Uncles and, it seemed, every youngster in the neighbourhood climbed aboard. There was great excitement as the charabanc moved away. For most of us this was the first trip in any sort of vehicle, let alone a trip to the seaside. Many of the children were accompanied only by Mothers or other female relative, Fathers were in short supply. The majority were still away, fighting either in France or at sea. My Father was unfit for war service, having a crippled leg. My Mother had died some two years earlier and Father had recently remarried. I think this trip was something in the nature of a celebration. There is no doubt I was fortunate to have been included in the outing.

My first sight of the sea on that hot Saturday morning in July 1918, struck me momentarily dumb. It looked so beautiful. I don't know how I imagined it as I played with other children in the back streets at home. Now, a somewhat scruffy nipper, I was looking at it for the first time as it shifted and glinted in the sun. The pier, as I remember, seemed to stretch to the horizon, with, at its end, a huge ocean going liner.

Directly the charabanc stopped, I could contain my excitement no longer. Without a word to my father or step-mother, I dashed off into the crowds and made my way to the edge of the water. I tore off my boots and stockings, slung them on the beach and waded into the sea. I was fascinated by everything I saw. I picked up cockles, dropping them for bigger and brighter shells. In turn I dropped them to pick up crabs and starfish.

Suddenly I realised that water was getting deeper, I looked towards the liner at the end of the pier. I looked back at the shore. It seemed miles away. How could I get to that big ship, without having to go back and find my way along the pier? The pier, it suddenly struck me, was quite close. I waded towards it and moved in and out among the supporting girders, calculating the chances of being able to climb up on to the pier itself.

The climb was easy enough. Every now and again I stopped to take another look at the liner, or to see if I could spot anyone I knew among the thousands who crowded the beach. At last I scrambled up to an opening between the railway lines which ran along the length of the pier.

I poked my head up through this gap, rested my hands on the sleepers, and looked down the line to see whether any trains were coming. I was turning to look the other way, when it happened. Suddenly I felt my limbs go rigid. It seemed that every part of me was trapped in a gigantic vice which was being slowly tightened. I could feel my face screw up, my eyes felt as though they were being forced out of my head from behind. I remember a blinding flash, then a crack like a rifle shot. Although I didn't know it, I had made contact with the live rail carrying more than two thousand volts. Hundreds of horrified holiday makers saw the flash, and, as the policeman told me later, saw me thrown from the pier down into about two feet of water.

The policeman waded out and brought me in, apparently dead. I was rushed to a nearby St. John's Ambulance Station, where after an hour of artificial respiration I came back to life. I felt somewhat shaken, but my only injuries it appeared, were a badly scorched right hand plus several cuts on my head. My clothes were handed to me, still warm from being dried in a nearby laundry. I was not detained, for under the circumstances it was thought better to let me go to search for someone who might know me.

They then discovered that I had no boots or socks (not uncommon in those days). I said I knew where I had left my boots and I hoped they might still be there. I tramped bare footed down to the sea-front. My head and hand were heavily bandaged. I was attracting quite a lot of attention. Someone asked me what I had done to myself and I proudly told my story. I was offered sweets, cakes, cups of tea and money. It was just when some generous and warm hearted old gentleman had offered to buy me a pair of shoes, that I was roughly seized, and I turned to be confronted by my angry father.

It appeared I had completely spoilt my parents' day out, rushing off like that. They had no idea what had happened to me, or even whether I knew where to pick up the charabanc for the return journey. I was so scared at first, I daren't tell the true story. I made out I had been knocked down in the road, but of course that story didn't account for my missing boots, so out came the truth.

I was marched back to the coach, where the story was retold to my step-mother. Her reaction was somewhat startling.

"That's right", she said, "Say you had been killed! Think of the expense it would have cost me and your father, to come down here to the inquest!". As a punishment, I had to go to school without those sympathy rousing bandages and, of course, no boots.

G.F.S.

Southend-on-Sea is the place I always turn to when I wish to revive happy memories of the seaside. It holds a very special place in my affections, for we never went anywhere else for a holiday throughout my childhood. It was so easy to get there by steam train on the L.M.S. railway from East London, and so cheap, which of course was the deciding factor.

We would be up at the crack of dawn on the day of departure. We used to set off with Dad carrying all our belongings in a light weight case. This was a kind of oblong straw-plaited basket, consisting of two identical halves one of which fitted over the top of the other and which were secured by leather straps. You never see such cases now, but they held a lot and were very useful if you happened to have a young baby, because one half, emptied, made a cosy crib.

We never stayed at hotels, nothing so grand. We booked up with a lady who lived in St Ann's Road. We had a room with cooking and attendance for £1 per week. We were expected to buy our own food and the landlady cooked it and served our meals. It was a perfectly satisfactory arrangement, which seemed to work well and provided us with a cheap holiday. We never went back to the house during the day, but we must have had wonderful summers then, for I never remember us walking about in the rain, or ever being cold and miserable. I only remember our sunburnt faces and the glow on our cheeks from the sea breezes and Southend's wonderful air, filled with ozone. Londoners swore by Southend's air to cure whooping-cough and chest troubles.

I remember one year, a open horse-drawn landau called every day at the house opposite to take the holiday-makers there wherever they might wish to go. I was under the impression that they were people of great wealth to be able to travel in such grand style. I wished that I could have just one ride in a landau, but I never did. We walked everywhere, "to stretch our legs," my Dad said.

I was permitted a ride down Southend's famous pier on the railway, which was of the toast-rack variety and very draughty, but I was never allowed to ride both ways - for reasons of economy, you may be sure. We even walked all the way to Shoeburyness, but we boarded a tram at the terminus at Thorpe Bay on the way back. We liked it best down towards Shoeburyness, because the beaches seemed wider and weren't so crowded. There were no houses at the seafront that end, and it was quiet and peaceful with not a car in sight, because Tom, Dick and Harry hadn't got around to owning such luxuries.

Occasionally, as a special treat, we would board one of the great big charabancs, new-fangled inventions, which stood in the roadway on the sea-front, just across from the Kursaal. The drivers would stand around shouting, touting for customers. A chalk-written message on a blackboard announced

"MYSTERY TOUR ONE SHILLING CHILDREN HALF PRICE"

We would climb up the steep steps, and sit down, glad of the chance to rest our feet and enjoy a bit of mystery at the same time. The charabanc was open to the winds of heaven, with a rain-hood which could be pulled up if it looked like being a wet day. We would be driven out into the countryside, where we would pull up at a pub for light refreshments. Then a photographer might appear and take our pictures as a little momento of our holiday. We were very pleased to buy them as no one seemed to carry cameras in those days.

Another treat was a trip in one of the large sailing boats which put out to sea with a great number of people aboard to see the sights. I remeber that, just after the 1914-1918 war, there were captured German liners lying at anchor, which were a great attraction. We also went on a boat trip to Canvey Island, which seemed like the land God forgot to me, just a few old shacks with corrugated iron roofs. I remember my mother's exact words as we landed and looked around. One glance at those shacks, and she remarked,

"What a dump!"

We were pleased to get in the boat and return to the delights of Southend.

I never saw such a place for eating houses as Southend. Garon's was the big name in restaurants in those days, and there were fish-and-chip bars galore, and those sausage and mash shops where you could see everything sizzling away in trays in the window. They always made me feel hungry. Then there were stalls loaded with piles of cockles, whelks and shrimps, and jellied eels. Southend has always been famous for its cockle teas. We used to go to

Cotgroves, just under the pier. A portrait of the founder hung on the wall, and his family gave swift and pleasant service. A cup of tea, plate of cockles, bread and butter cost only sixpence the lot, and you were given such a warm welcome when you walked in. There were smiles all round. They were an old-fashioned family firm who valued their customers. That was why we always returned.

Yet another treat was a visit to the 'Jolly Boys'. They held their concerts in as large marquee on the sea-front, with the performers singing and dancing in their pierrot costumes. We would watch Punch and Judy shows down on the beach, and we listened to religious fanatics and soap-box orators spouting away on the crowded pavements opposite the Kursaal. (I think that they chose that particular spot because the public lavatories were there - with everyone popping in and out they were sure of a good audience.) My father seemed to glean some amusement from them and would laugh away to himself as they worked themselves up into a frenzy. There was more laughter when we visited the Hall of Mirrors inside the Kursaal and gazed at our distorted images. There was so much to see and to enjoy at Southend-on-Sea.

There were some tearful times, too, in Southend. When I was small, my father set me up on his shoulders because I was tired, then passed under a shop blind in the High Street and caused me to collect a large bump on my forehead through coming in contact with the iron support. On another occasion I fell off a woodern jetty and made a spectacular splash into the sea. How scared I have been of water ever since! Then there was the day we visited a tea-shop in Thorpe Bay, and my father's big feet kicked over the little bucket I had placed so carefully under the table. He not only spilled the sea water therein, but caused a whole regiment of crabs to go scurrying for safety and freedom. Oh! the wails that went up. Not only from me, but from the shopkeeper too. He wasn't very pleased.

One thing we did enjoy were the lovely walks around the outskirts of the town. Southend wasn't the great built-up place then that it is now. Once through Prittlewell village, we would be out in the countryside and could roam about cornfields to our heart's delight. There was also lovely Priory Park to explore, and the park at Southchurch with its small childrens zoo. I never see Californian poppies opening in the sun, without remembering Southchurch Park, where I first saw them growing.

Walks out over the mud were always popular. Old ladies with corns and callouses said it made their feet feel lovely. Lots of children wore rope-soled paddling shoes with canvas tops and tapes that tied round the ankles to keep them on. They were the fore-runners of todays flip-flops, designed to protect little feet from stones and the cockle, mussel and winkle shells that lay about in such profusion.

Southend's muddy foreshore was a fascinating place, full of interest for the young. There were little pools full of tiny silvery fish, crabs galore, shells and seaweed of all kinds, even a starfish or two if we were lucky. I loved it. Once we got past the muddy part, we came to beautiful firm sand, and eventually we reached the sea. It would be coming in so slowly, running over our toes warm and gentle as a caress. It sparkled and glinted in the sun like diamonds, and we would be so far out from the shore that the multitudes were left behind, and there was no sound to disturb the peace except the soft lap of little wavelets and the sea-birds calling.

Strange that Southend, with its teeming humanity out on the spree, could also offer such tranquillity, such inner happiness and contentment and the feeling that "God's in his heaven all's right with the world". But that is what going out in the estuary did for me. I would look around all the space of sea and sky and feel as free as the sea-birds who flew there.

Our seven days always went so quickly, and then we would be on the train once more, with the engine huffing and puffing and sending out great clouds of steam. Then we would be off. Back to grimy East London, not forgetting a straw bag of cockles for Grandma and a few sticks of rock for little friends. I always kept my nose pressed against the window-pane in order to catch a last glimpse of the sea and all the little boats bobbing about. After we passed the ruins of Hadleigh castle and the old house-boats stuck in the mud at Benfleet Creek, I knew it was really goodbye. Dear Southend, how I loved you! For there were none so well equipped to appreciate your charms as those children who lived out their lives in the drabness of London's little back streets. To us you were a Seventh Heaven!

M.B.

Now was the chance of a working holiday. Our neighbour had taken a house at Thorpe Bay, Southend. It was to be a boarding house. As I had never had a holiday, my neighbour asked me if I would like to visit them, but I would have to work for my keep. I then had three children, so of course I had to take them with me too. It meant waiting at table, making beds, doing bedrooms, washing and washing up. So I really did earn our keep. Though I must say that she paid our fares there and back.

We stayed three weeks. I was able to get to the beach sometimes, and the girls loved it. That's all they could do, as money was very scarce.

There was an old man who had a room at the top of the stairs. He was a permanent guest. He had so much money, it just used to fall out of his pockets. When I went to tidy his room, I was always finding money on the chairs, under the bed. I would pick it up and leave it on the bedside cabinet. All the times I gave it back to him saying,

"You dropped this, Mr Jackson," but never a smile or a thank-you, just a grunt.

One day while I was washing his shirts, something fell out and stuck to my foot. It was three sopping wet pound notes. Of all the days I was tempted, that was the day. So I hung out his shirts, and the girls were in the garden with me - I know it was wrong, but I so much wanted to give them a little treat, and I had no money of my own - it was like manna from heaven.

So I took them along to the Front, and we all had fish and chips, that have never tasted so good before or since. Then I bought them all some socks, a toy and some stockings for myself. My neighbour never knew, but I felt awful because I knew that he knew I had nothing.

We walked along the beach. It was a

lovely fresh night and, although I felt tired, the cool breeze seemed to put new life into me. The girls faces were fresh and glowing, not that pale look they always seemed to have in London. I think if Mr Jackson had seen the girls' faces when they were enjoying their fish and chips, he must surely have thought it was worth three pounds.

Anyway I think it was worth it for all the hard work. I have given that three pound back a thousand times. I have brought up a big family. I have done lots of charity work over the years and still sing at concerts to help raise funds for pensioners' parcels at Christmas.

We stayed the three weeks and then returned to London. I know this isn't much of a story, but I have done my best.

D.B.

Chapter V
"The longest day . . . "

I remember that hot, summer day in August better than yesterday or the happenings of last week.

Such a long way back - I was almost ten years old and enjoying the holidays in the constant companionship of my cousins, who lived a stone's throw distant, as most of my relatives seemed to do in those days. We had been blessed with a wonderful spell of summer weather, and I was finding the world full of delights. We were usually packed off immediately after breakfast to Highgate Woods or the wild, broad stetches of glorious Hampstead Heath. Our mothers took it in turns to fill our canvas lunch bags with potato scones, and small, sweet tomatoes with tiny twists of salt, jam sandwiches and a bottle of homemade lemonade. We were supposed to eke out this fare, but usually ate the lot at the first opportunity thus leaving ourselves free for climbing trees, assaulting other children who fancied the same tree and generally running wild, as Grandfather put it. He told me that I was 'all legs and hair', which I took as a deep insult.

Now, I had been promised something

special. I was to spend a few days with my Uncle George's family in Stamford Hill, North London. I was to take the tram, all by myself, from the end of Hornsey Road.

I was faintly nervous. I did not know Uncle George's wife, or his three children very well. My uncle was a soldier and had spent much of his time in India, Africa, Egypt. He was now on something called 'extended leave', and to add to the family excitement had actually purchased a house, the first of all Grandfather's sons and daughters to do such a fine thing.

Grandfather had six sons and six daughters. His wife had died at the birth of the last, Aunt Dolly, named thus because she was so tiny. Once, when my mother was telling a friend about it, my father was heard to murmur,

"Small wonder!"

This upset my mother, so he had to go out and buy a bag of her favourite sweets, a sort of scarlet jelly, with chopped almonds. I liked to watch my father coaxing my mother back into her usual good humour. It made her look young and pretty, and my father loving but masterful, like people in a story.

Well, no one met me at the tram stop that day, but I soon found the road. There were not many proper streets or houses there at all. Some builders workmen gave me directions, and suddenly, there it was! The only completed house in all those empty fields. No one had told me Uncle George lived in the country. And this was country! You had only to look around and the green earthy mounds, the clumps of thick grass, and that single white house, now only a few feet away. What fun was waiting for me in these blissful surroundings?

I pushed open the front gate, but had hardly set foot on the tiled path when the door opened and I was all but flattened by the combined assault of Albert, Molly and Violet. Uncle George has said they were boisterous. I thought that was an under-estimate.

Aunt Louise looked delicate, yet had weathered many years of travelling and child-bearing in strange places. I never saw her do any rough house-work, then, or at any time after. She seemed to leave all of that to a lady they called Grandma. Grandma was a stout, grim-faced little woman who spent all her time in the large kitchen communicating with the rest of us only through the serving hatch. She certainly dished up a splendid early lunch (as they called it. It was "dinner" to us at home.)

Then we were told to make the most of the sunshine, and stay out in the fields till the workmen went home and tea would be ready. I could scarcely believe that it was barely midday as we ran like lunatics down the path, round the back of the house, and headed for the sandy hillocks, the tough green grass, untouched, as yet, by the builders.

Oh glory! Would there ever again be such a beautiful day? I thought, with my usual magnifying of events. I had a wild, overwhelming imagination that I lived with happily enough. My Godfather, Uncle William said it was a "dangerous thing". I do not think I ever knew what he meant. I was an 'only' child, and believe that it is not uncommon to live a great deal in a kind of dream world.

Within half an hour I had torn my new petticoat, lost my hair ribbon, scuffed my sandals and cut my knee not inconsiderably. Albert bound it up, roughly, impatiently with his grimy handkerchief as Molly and Violet waited, jumping up and down, eager to get on with the game. Later, when we had sprawled on the gritty soil to catch our breath, I saw that the red blood had seeped through the handkerchief. I felt a bit sick staring down at it, but Albert was scornful,

"You don't need to be scared of a bit of blood. Our bodies are full of it, gallon! You've heaps to spare."

I could not fault his logic but thought how gently my mother would have tended the injury. Suddenly, I missed my own home and it's comfortable, familiar ways. Then, there in the distance we saw Grandma, waving, puffing her way towards our camp. It could not be that we were late for tea. So we waited until she reached us, hand pressed to bosom, fighting for breath. I held mine, in sympathy.

"You've to come home, at once! Your father's gone to London, and goodness knows when we'll see him again, but he says you're to do exactly as your mother tells you. So, come along now."

I saw Albert open his mouth prepared to protest or argue. Something held him silent. We were all scared, I think, though we couldn't puzzle out why. As we trudged along behind Grandma, I had a sudden conviction that it would be a long time before I ran in those halcyon fields again.

We were given a hasty meal, ham sandwiches, then scones and jam with cold milk. Casting furtive glances at one another over our tall glasses, we refrained from troubling Aunt Louise, who had begged us not to ask 'silly questions', she would explain it all. Something very serious had taken their father to London. No, no one was dead, nothing like that. She placed her thin, veined hand on my shoulder as we remained sitting around the table.

"Poor Frances," she said, "And you have only just come. I'm sorry, but you have to go home, child. Albert will see you to the tram stop. I have already packed your case, but run upstairs and see if I have missed anything".

She looked around, distracted as though seeking support in trying circumstances, and I felt a twinge of pity for her. But not as much as I did for myself. I felt the tears prickling in my eyes and, turning away as quickly as I could, I ran upstairs to the bedroom which I was to have shared with the two girls.

Oh, it was cruel, cruel! And it had been so beautiful until now. I could hear Grandma downstairs in the kitchen. It sounded as though she had become intent on smashing all the crockery at once. Perhaps she was terribly angry? Well, I had done nothing wrong. Why send me home?

Within ten minutes, Albert and I started off down the road, he carrying my suitcase, showing off a bit, but there was no one to see, even the noisy workmen had vanished from the face of the earth. Strangest of all, I did not hear one bird singing in all those leafy trees. I began to walk faster. I wanted to be home. I wanted to be with the people who loved me most.

Trying to settle comfortably on the hard, slippery tram seat, I sat with my eyes downcast, afraid that the misery I felt would be obvious to the other passengers. I just kept hoping that the unspilled tears in my eyes would dry quickly, and not run down my cheeks to shame me. I had to look up, however, as we neared my stop. No one was looking at me. They kept up a constant, shrill chatter, mouths moving, heads shaking, nodding. I might have been invisible.

Alighting at the corner of Hornsey Road, I almost ran until I reached Grove Road, where my favourite sweet shop was. I would treat myself to a chocolate covered macaroon. When I reached the toy shop, I stared up, as I must have done a dozen times in the past two weeks, at the orange painted scooter hanging high above the door, praying silently that I would be given it for my birthday in a months time. It was seven shillings and sixpence, if you can recall that kind of money.

I turned, and knocked against the heavy board displaying the latest STOP PRESS! announcement. There was only one word there "WAR!"

I finished off my macaroon and turned the corner into our street. I was thinking how triumphant my Grandfather would be, telling us all how right he had been about the war. He meant with the Germans, and especially Kaiser Bill, their King. Who was in the war on those placards I did not know. You could see wars at the cinema every Saturday. The soldiers wore dashing uniforms and stood stalwart to the end. The good people always won. We left content and happy.

I was within sight of my house. I

sighed. The place would be full of visitors. It always was. Mother had five sisters and six brothers, most of whom lived locally. Three of the boys were soldiers. "Regulars", they were called. Uncle George, Uncle Tom and Uncle William. The last two were on leave and were certain to be in the kitchen, sampling my mother's scones. They were always hungry.

I stood just inside the gate, unable to believe my eyes. The house was curtainless,the Venetian blinds all fully drawn. There was a poster across one window, "FOR SALE OR LET". I shut my eyes, telling myself that I was dreaming, but when I opened them it was just the same. I kept on knocking for about five minutes, on and off. The side gate was fastened securely so that I was unable to get into the rear garden. Nothing. Only silence. I walked across the tiny patch of grass before the front window and peered inside. It was empty; no tables, chairs, piano, pictures, sofa. I remember holding my mouth so as not to scream. I sometimes had nightmares. It was like that then.

Was this the secret catastrophe that had driven me from Stamford Hill? So ghastly that they had not dared tell me? I heard a clatter.

I turned. looking upwards, and there was the woman who lived next door leaning from a window. She looked flushed, busy, impatient but kindly.

"Oh, it's you, ducks! No use keeping up that row, they're not there! Didn't your Ma tell you where they was all going?"

I shook my head. speechless with fright.

"Well I never! It was sudden, like. I thought you was away for a week". She hesitated, then took a scrap of paper from her apron pocket. "Here, I've the address. It's in Hornsey Road. You must have passed it if you came by tram, Number 322. Remember that, 322. It's opposite the ironmonger's on the corner, and right next to that little tailor."

I thanked her, said the number aloud a few times at her request, then, turning away, started back along the way I had so recently come.

My feelings were all jumbled up inside me. Relief that they had not all been murdered, or something equally horrible, but anger, outrage, self-pity, mingled with a sensation like excitement. I would never, never forgive my mother for moving without telling me. Grown up people did such beastly things sometimes, far worse than anything children ever did!

I had to stand by the kerb for a long time, waiting for the red, open-decked 'bus, the horses and carts, and two barrow boys to pass before I could cross safely. It was a main road with lots of shops and offices and tall houses in between. The houses looked elegant but neglected, with paint peeling from upper window-sills and unkempt front gardens. I reached number 322, and put my hands for the first time on the sturdy, carved iron gates that opened on to the cracked mosaic path. Dragon Gates, all the years I lived there I called them that. If no one were watching I would caress them, enjoying the sharp metal and even the odour of ingrained grease and grime.

I banged the knocker three or four times. A voice shouted for me to come in. The hall was cluttered with odd pieces of our furniture. I tripped down a deep, unnoticed step.

My mother was laying the table. She smiled at me immediately, just as if everything was alright with the world.

"Well, so you're back. I thought Louise would decide it was best." I was flooded with resentment. I felt hot and angry.

"You all moved without telling me! You never tell me anything, never!"

I think she was suprised. She looked guilty, and was about to speak when Uncle William came in. He explained that my mother had wished to suprise me, but that now things were all topsy-turvy anyway, with old George having to rush off, and goodness knows when he would be sent for himself. His words did not register much. My mother came close and I allowed her to kiss me and stroke my head, as I glanced with rising interest round this new kitchen.

The walls were wooden, a pale pine I think. The sunlight from outside made them golden. High up on the wall there was a row of gleaming bells. I wondered what they were for. I wanted to ask Mother, but in came my grandfather, waving his stick before him, making his way to his familiar armchair positioned now by a gleaming black stove which took up a half of the wall.

He glared at me, and I thought,

"What have I done ?"

He had a sharp temper and could make you feel like a small insect with his lashing tongue. I loved him, very much.

"Didn't I tell you, my girl, over and over that it would all start in the Balkans? No one listens to me!"

Ashamed before my uncle, I hung my head. Uncle William said, gruffly,

"Give it a rest Father, or you'll frighten us all!"

The old man flashed his bright blue eyes at each of us in turn.

"You do well to be scared my boy! There'll be George and Tom and you over there, and me not knowing what's happening from day to day...I can tell you, Will, I wish I were going with you!"

At that moment my uncle Tom. the youngest of Grandfather's sons, clattered down that deep step. He burst out laughing when Uncle William said fervently,

"Thank God you're not coming with us, Father!"

I could not see anything funny about their conversation, but every one else was grinning, except Grandfather, who sat in his chair and scowled. I wanted to escape. I hurried past my mother, through the capacious scullery and into the garden. I was brought up short by the ivy-covered shed close to the back door.

Skirting this, I stared at my new surroundings. The garden was mainly grass, neglected and scorched by the recent long spell of sunshine. To one side was a rose bush, its pink petals over-blown, dropping onto the narrow path. I kicked at them, and scented their delicate fragrance. Suddenly, happily, I thought of the orange painted scooter, hanging above the poster. WAR! Even a war couldn't spoil my hopes in that direction, could it?

The garden was long. At the bottom was a fairly low wall over which I saw a large ugly building. It had lots of tiny windows, some barred. Later I asked my mother what it was. She told me it was an orphanage, and Grandfather broke in, bitterly, saying that they would need room for a lot more orphans now we were at war. I had not fully realised that we were at war until then. But I had seen films about orphans at the cinema, and was sure that they always ended up adopted by rich and kindly people, whatever their previous misfortunes. So that would be all right.

I went to bed in a my strange bedroom. There were pretty pink-flowered curtains at the little window, but I said nothing. I was still hurt that they had moved without telling me. I did accept Mother's contrite kiss as she tucked me in. I was waiting for my father to come and hug his special good night. Whatever the time, he always did.

He worked long hours for a coach builder. When he was a young man, a heavy coach body had fallen and crushed him, causing his slight lameness. The extra effort to walk made him tired. How I loved easing off his tough boots and handing him his slippers if I happened to be up late.

Though I was exhausted, sleep that night was long in coming. So much had happened. I felt emotionally battered by my experiences. Events were jumbled together, passing before my weary eyes like crazy images on a flickering screen: Stamford Hill, not far off, but just like the real country, the brilliant sunshine, the sandy hillocks, the rough grass that smelled earthy and nice when you rolled over and over, Aunt Louise's mournful eyes, and the sudden departure of Uncle George. I would never forget the shock of feeling abandoned before that empty house. It had been the longest day of my life.

In my imagination, I still heard Grandma banging crockery and pans in that Stamford Hill kitchen, venting her rage on someone, something. My lips stretched into a wavery smile, staying there as if the skin, like myself, was too fatigued to move any more. I decided, God help me! in my ignorance or innocence, that even if we were at war, it would make little difference. Things like that always happened in far off places, and the fighting looked rather splendid at the cinema.

I said my prayers for the second time. I felt that it would not be right to pray for that orange scooter, yet I longed to be given it for my birthday. I thought of it, hard, and kept my fingers crossed.

I said sorry for feeling jealous when Mother had said she was worried about 'her' boys.

"They're not your children!" I had muttered resentfully. She had given me a sad, sad look, and I had turned my back on her. That was, I think, the worst thing I did on that memorable day.

August 1914 it was. The prelude to

suffering and disaster had come to our family in a blaze of brilliant sunshine and blue skies. I went to sleep, eventually, still unknowing.

V.R.

Chapter VI

"If the roof falls in I want to keep the dust out of my eyes . . . "

That night when the Zeppelin was attacked, all the neighbours were out in their gardens watching as it drifted overhead. It was like a blazing cigar as it neared its last resting place, and landed, an inferno, near the junction of Outward Common Road and Jackson's Lane, Billericay. The man next door was jumping up and down, his arms raised high above his head, as he shouted,

"Frizzle, you bs___, frizzle, you b___s"

In later years, when Dad retired, we moved from East Ham to Laindon, just a couple of miles from where the victims were buried in Great Burstead churchyard. I have paid many visits to the graves, the stones of which listed the names and rank of the twenty-two crew of the Zeppelin. On the anniversary of its destruction, a German crew used to visit and lay wreaths on its tiny piece of garden, even up to 1939 and the outbreak of the Second World War. (The bodies have since been transferred to the German Military Cemetary in Staffordshire.)

Another childhood memory of the 1914-1918 war is that of my mother during an air-raid. She would sit in a corner of the bedroom with a coat over her head. When I asked the reason for this, her reply was,

"If the roof falls in, I want to keep the dust out of my eyes."

H.H.

We used to keep our toys in a box beneath the big Dutch dresser which my father had made. My brother George had already been called into the Army, and a cousin had been taken prisoner by the Huns. How I hated them! Two of my sisters were working at Keiller's in Silvertown, May in the factory, Gladys in the office. I had not long started school.

We had finished our evening meal which Mum always gave us before the 'workers' came home, and she had told us to put our toys away for it was almost time to go to bed. Suddenly there was a great bang and the house seemed to shake. I hit my head on the dresser and cried. Mum rubbed the place to ease the pain. The air seemed to smell of fire, and the sky was red with flames and smoke. Then my sisters appeared, turning the corner, and Mum sighed with relief.

"What has happened? Was it a bomb?" she asked. "The air-raid policemen hasn't come by!"

He was an ordinary copper who would cycle along the roads wearing his helmet, and shouting 'Take Cover!'

"We got as far as the Tidal Basin Station, when someone yelled,'Run as fast as you can!'. So we did." Gladys breathlessly told us. "Then there was a big bang and ..look at the sky!"

Mushrooming clouds spread from the South, where there was a bright red glow that increased in size.

"What's happened?" called a neighbour.

"Explosion at the munitions factory!" said a man who looked like a sweep. "I got covered with soot. You watch out! The blighters will be over tonight for they'll have that light to guide them."

He was right. Before Gladys and May had finished their meal, the 'maroon', a cannon fired at Woolwich Arsenal, warned us of the enemy's approach. Mum had put a mattress under the kitchen table (another result of Dad's handicraft), and we children would sit there until the 'All Clear' sounded. Gladys read us a story from a book which she had won as a school prize. The story was about two little German girls who had lost their parents and had been sent to live in England with an Aunt. Each time a bomb fell, the house shook. It still stood, but I hated the Germans then.

Later that year they tried daylight raids and we stood in our back garden watching our plane circling a Zeppelin. As the fabric started to burn, men jumped clear of the flames, some with their clothing already on fire. They were men, like my brother who was 'somewhere in France', real men who perhaps had little sisters waiting for them at home. They had been ordered to fly that Zeppelin. They had no choice for they would be shot if they disobeyed the Kaiser's orders. What was it all about? Why were the Germans bombing our cities?

I did not know then, but later discovered that, because his mother was Queen Victoria's eldest child, Kaiser Wilhelm thought that he should be King of England. That raid was unexpected following the explosion, and, though the Second World War was much worse, I never forgot that first raid.

A.E.R.

I had recently left school in August, 1917, when on a beautiful Sunday evening, twenty enemy Gothas made a sneak raid on Southend and thirty five people, including a school friend, were killed, and a vast number injured. Unlike Southend in the second war, when half the town was evacuated, there were no restrictions on visitors between 1914 and 1918. Consequently they arrived in their thousands every summer weekend and on the Sunday in question, crowds were making their way to Victoria Railway Station, when the first aerial torpedoes were released by the raiders. My parents, sisters and I were outside our house when the German planes appeared, and as there was no firing by our batteries, we watched and wondered if they were really friendly. Suddenly there was a shrill piercing noise and the terrific explosion of the first bomb. Neighbours joined us as we rushed indoors while all hell seemed to be let loose.

Between Victoria Circus and the Railway Station were private houses, the Gem Cinema, rows of shops and coal offices. It was here that the first bomb fell and 18 people were killed — a young man, arm in arm with his fiancee and on their way to a Salvation Army meeting, became mutilated bodies. The raid lasted only a few minutes but the damage and casualties were tremendous. I rushed to Victoria Circus by cycle and saw firemen hosing away blood and flesh, while ambulance workers and police collected human remains. The nine fatalities in the Guildford Road and Milton Street area included Fred Hawes, a class mate of mine, his mother and her young niece. A colleague of my Father's , Mr. Robert West, a cripple, was dragged from the ruins of his house but his wife and thirteen year old daughter were killed.

There were, of course, many more wartime happenings. Strangely it was my Mother who took me to two events which will always remain in my memory. The first was to Victoria Station soon after the war had started, to see the first Belgian wounded arrive in Southend. For me it was a new experience to be out of bed at midnight. We joined the crowds who waited outside the station, and cheered as each ambulance or car conveyed our wounded allies to the Palace Hotel(which had been converted into Queen Mary's Royal Naval Hospital.) We could see that some of the wounded were in a bad state. It was a harrowing experience yet I think Mum was right to give me my first lesson in the suffering and tragedy of war.

Later we were to have happier ways of meeting the wounded, (not only Belgian). They used to drop long pieces of string from the balconies of the hotel-hospital, and we attached gifts to the ends. My sister and I like many children, but far more adults, took packets of

Woodbines or Player's Weights, and more expensive gifts, all of which were gratefully accepted.

There was excitement on another night, when there were anti-German riots in Southend. Hooligan gangs smashed up shops with German sounding names-boards. Many of the shop-keepers had lived in England a good many years, and in no way would have impeded the allies' war effort. Dozens of shopfronts were smashed and goods looted, but the police and military acted quickly. I saw one looter being frog-marched to the police station. It was my first experience of civil disobedience, and although many arrests were made and sentences imposed, the tradesmen never recovered their losses. Indeed some may have been interned on the liners which lay off the pier and were used as prisons.

A big house in Victoria Avenue, which later became a high school, housed many German Officer prisoners. A number of German service men and civilians died while in captivity and were buried, at first, in Sutton Road cemetary. I went to the funeral of one. The coffin, covered with the German flag, was drawn to the cemetery on a gun carriage. On it rested flowers from the dead man's friends, and from his British Army guards. A German pastor read the burial service, the Last Post was sounded and, to the dead man enemy, soldiers - British - fired a salvo of shots over the grave. They were the last bullets to be fired over that German- shots not fired in the hatred of war, but in tribute to one caught up in it.

A.P.G.

I was just coming up to four years old and living in North London when war broke out, but I cannot recall any excitements or incidents that accompanied this event. There were certain happenings at that time in my life that do remain clear, so it is not a case of being too young to remember. One occurrence which has remained a complete blank in my mind, was the departure of my father to join the armed services in 1916. I just cannot remember him being there, coming home from work each day, settling down to meals and family life, and then suddenly not being there.

Perhaps the most dramatic event that we experienced whilst still living in London, was the great daylight raid in 1917. It was a Saturday morning, and I and my sister Doris and younger brother Eric, were playing indoors at the rear of the house when I became aware that my mother was suddenly in a state of alarm. I now noticed a loud, slowly increasing sound of heavy engines approaching from the front of the house Obviously it was this that had alarmed my mother. We were told to sit still whilst my mother went to the front door to look out. She immediately banged the door shut again, and ran back to us exclaiming

"It's the Germans".

Although only a six year old, I had inevitably absorbed some of the current feeling about "The Germans", those hateful, cruel and wholly obnoxious beings often known in conversation as "Jerries" or sometimes "Huns", who, over the sea somewhere, were wreaking their awful deeds on innocent civilians and our soldiers.

But what were they doing out there in front of our house? No wonder there was alarm!

We were hurriedly gathered into the kitchen huddling close together while the roar of the engines passed overhead. It was, of course, the great daylight raid carried out by a number of German Gotha planes which I have often read about since. (I wish I had gone to the front door with my mother to have seen those fearsome looking machines approaching in the sky towards us). In later years my mother often related the story but

clearly lost none of its traumatic impact.

Soon after the aeroplanes had passed over there were several loud explosions, not all that far away. The reason for my mother's sudden alarm was now apparent. It was a completely new dimension in life with the enemy among us. Previously I had imagined that they were far away in foreign places - so far away that it was difficult to believe.

The bombs soon ceased, the noise of the planes receded, and we figuratively and literally unwound ourselves from the tense embraces we had assumed during the period of crisis. The next day we were taken by my mother, (to the Seven Sisters Road area I believe) to view the damage done by the bombs.

It was not long after this, that my mother decided to move from London to Dedham where she had spent her schooldays and her parents and sisters still lived. In those days there were always several cottages available to let at around two shillings per week. It was not long before we were tenants of a cottage, or rather one corner of a large house sub-divided into four dwellings, on Dedham Heath.

It might have been thought that the war would have little impact on the quiet village of Dedham on the Essex/Suffolk border, but although its intrusions were less common, and less expected, they were no less dramatic. Dedham is about twenty miles from Harwich, and from the Heath it is possible on a clear day, to see the Stour Estuary as it winds out to the port of Harwich, and the North Sea beyond.

On clear nights it was possible to see flashing lights in the estuary which, as I was informed by a sailor uncle home on leave, were Morse Code signals emanating from ships or shore establishments at Harwich. I recall a sense of disappointment, and perhaps disillusion, when Uncle Cecil confessed that he was unable to read the message being transmitted. It could not have been very vital information they were sending, if it was possible for it to be read (if not by Uncle Cecil) by anyone along the Stour Valley. But it added a little excitement and glamour to the scene, as we walked up Castle Hill to our home on the Heath. The flashing signals gave a suggestion of activity and mighty deeds being done in the waging of the war. (This was probably quite unjustified.)

One day - it was towards the end of the war - I was walking alone down the footpath across the back fields leading to East Lane when I found myself confronted by a stranger in 'my' cherished fields, a stranger dressed in smart city type clothes quite out of place out in the fields. We were both startled at the sudden encounter, and without a word I veered off down the hedge to avoid the necessity of crossing the stile where he was standing. What intrigued me particularly was the fact that, when I first saw him, he was looking across the valley towards Harwich through a pair of binoculars. Was he, I wonder, a real spy? Had I come across one of those beings, sinister or glamorous, depending on which side they are on. I mentioned the incident to no-one, nor have I ever done so In fact this is the very first revelation I have made of the episode. It was probably quite harmless.

Although I cannot remember the war beginning, I clearly remember the excitement and relief which followed the talk of an "Armistice" -a word which I quickly learned meant that the fighting was coming to an end. It also meant that the men would be coming home again. Those glamorous, high-spirited beings, who had occasionally and briefly appeared among us bedecked in navy-blue or khaki, were becoming ordinary men, working at the mill, or on the land, or were associated with new style of life known as being "on the dole".

My father came home too. I had seen very little of him for the last three or four years. Maybe I resented his homecoming at first. As the eldest son, I had been 'acting' man of the house for so long. We adjusted to our new regime in due course.

The day my Father returned home from the War, holds special memories. and not merely because of his return to the family circle. In view of the importance of the occasion, my Mother had hired a taxi to meet him at Ardleigh Railway Station. It was a model T open-topped Ford, which is easy to remember, because it was at that time the only car in the village.

Some time later, preparations began to be made for the Great Peace Celebration. We noticed the gathering of huge amounts of material for a bonfire on Hewittes Meadow, where the Annual Flower Show was usually held. It must have been the biggest pile of combustible material in the area since the approach of the Spanish Armada.

At last the great day of the Peace Celebration came. Very early I was down in the street to make sure I missed nothing. I cannot remember what the day's programme involved, but I do recall seeing the ex-servicemen of the village gathering in The Square. Some were in fancy dress. They carried a variety of musical instruments, some of them mere 'Kazoos' or comb and paper, and set out on a round tour of the village, ostensibly to emphasise the glad news that they were safely home from the war and peace now reigned, but with the main motive. I suspect, of collecting enough money to permit an uninhibited drinking spree later in the day.

As well as calling at every house, all the pubs on the way round were visited. However the highlight of the day, for me, was the great bonfire and the firework display which began as soon as darkness fell.

The excitement of the tremendous burning pile, frequent explosions of fireworks, and the occasional squeals as a Chinese Cracker found its way into the centre of the onlookers, may have given us a feeling that something unpleasant and sinister was being purged by the fire, and the gaiety of the crowds where, for the first time in many years the whole village was gathered together - wives, husbands, children, the old and the young of all classes.

Meanwhile the bonfire raged, the fireworks earned frequent 'Ooohs' as they decorated the night sky and the joy became less confined. The bonfire contained at least one barrel of tar and the effect was tremendous.

The barrels of beer bought from the proceeds of the days collection were in constant use. There was a sudden flurry of excitement and alarm when Uncle Bert (my father's uncle actually) was pushed at great speed round and round the perimeter of the bonfire, propelled by another ex-soldier (equally well intoxicated), in the wheelbarrow that had been provided to bring up the beer barrels . Aunt Flo (Uncle Bert's wife) yelled and screamed for him to desist, especially when the barrow sometimes approached within a few feet of the burning material, but Uncle Bert was oblivious to any danger, deleriously happy in his alcoholic haze and every reason to be so.

He had survived several years of active service, and was now back home with his family, with a job in the village and the opportunity to meet his mates down at the pub or on the allotment. He could become a normal citizen once again.

He had every reason to be happy. So did most of the other men and women on the field that evening and perhaps we can be forgiving for the exuberance of their celebrations.

Away on the horizen the sky was reddened by the effect of another village bonfire celebrating its relief from the horrors and privations of the past few years. I think it was at Langham, but it may have been Stratford St. Mary. And so we all went home, the excitements were over and normal life ready to be resumed.

There was one more public event connected with the war. This was the unveiling of the War Memorial in The Square - where it still stands today (With the sad addition of several more names to follow those that lost their lives in the "War to end all Wars"). All the villagers attended the ceremony of dedication, everyone dressed in their Sunday best clothes. The whole affair was very decorous and vastly different to the wild day of rejoicing of the previous year. Perhaps a fitting conclusion.

P.A.L.B.

We were a family of five children living in Surrey on the edge of an open common. Life seemed to go on quite normally for us until 1916, when my Father was called up. Before that year I can only remember taking part in a school concert which we gave for wounded soldiers. I was rather intrigued by all those men being dressed alike in bright blue suits with white shirts and red ties, but I am sure I had no conception of why they were there, or how they came to be wounded. I knew the war was in France, and that they crossed the English Channel to get there, and that they lived in muddy trenches, but that was another world. From time to time we heard booming noises and we were told that they were the guns in France.

The day came when my Father had to go. My Mother was terribly distraught and the bottom seemed to fall out of life in the home. But it was August and summer holidays from school. We went out looking for dragon flies and stag beetles, newts and frogs and toads as usual. It was only at night that we realised that things had changed. My Father came home at first in mufti and said that he had been marching somewhere in London all day, but after a few days he came home in khaki with horrid putties wound round his legs, a greatcoat which was too long for him and a nasty peaked cap over his eyes. He had lots of brass buttons which had to be polished without getting white stuff on his coat. The Army gave him a button stick to do this, which we children thought was very cute. He did not come home for long. He was sent to Aldershot and only came home on leave after that. We settled down to wait for the postman every morning.

Both my parents were great gardeners. We grew all our own fruit and vegetables, so my Mother taught us older children to weed and hoe and harvest the crops, so that all would be in order when Father came back.

In March 1917 my Father was sent to France and we began making up prcels of things he liked. I had to take them to the Post Office about one mile from our house. I had just learnt to make a Yorkshire Parkin and so this had to be included. I can remember my Mother making a sort of chocolate from cocoa butter for the parcel. It was poured into tin lids to set. We never knew what happened to these parcels, as in May 1917 my father was reported missing and that was the last we heard of him. During those three months, we children used to go to the bedroom window when we knew that the postman was coming down the road, so to be the first to report that there was a letter from Dad. Unfortunately it never came. My mother advertised for information in the Territorial Gazette. I can remember a soldier coming to see us and saying that he was with my father when he was shot in the face. My mother always seemed very sceptical about this and so we never felt that we really knew what had happened. We cannot be suprised when we read the terrible history of those battles today.

I can remember a night when we looked across the sky, and saw the Zeppelin coming down in flames over Potter's Bar. I asked my mother if there were men in it. When she said that there were, a chill horror came over me, a horror that remains with me to this day, man's inhumanity to man.

Perhaps my last memory of the First World War is of November 11th 1918. There was little going on in our district, but we heard of the rejoicing and celebrations in London. My mother felt that she had lost so much, and was now face with the prospect of bringing up five children alone, that there was little rejoicing in our house. It was a sad day for us. I have found it a sad day ever since. Man seems to have learned so little from it. The Cenotaph was erected in london in the memory of the men who fell. If those men could rise up on Armistice Day, would they feel they had made the great sacrifice in vain? I wonder.

M.S.

Chapter VII

"These two rabbits should come in handy for Christmas . . ."

In the hinterland of one's mind, Christmas memories loom large. The magic of childhood Christmases remains with us through all the vicissitudes of later years. The one that has haunted me, the delight being ever new, is the Christmas of 1916.

The Great War was raging, my Father was in Flanders, and we were poor. I was seven years of age and my sister was five. Mother was in receipt of an Army pittance to keep us, and Christmas, and all it meant, looked pretty bleak and drear. I remember looking in at the toys in the shop windows, the lovely engines, cranes and other boyhood joys, all beyond my eager little hands.

Christmas Eve dawned cold and miserable, with a persistent drizzle falling. We were huddled in front of the fire when a knock came on the door, causing us to rise with anticipation, for we had so few callers. When my Mother opened the door, a soldier stood there carrying two large dead rabbits by the hind legs. We were all excited, thinking for a moment it was Dad.

"Mrs. Elmer?" began the soldier," I am

serving with your husband in France, and he asked me to call. These two rabbits should be handy for Christmas." After this big, red faced soldier had sat down to a cup of tea, he fascinated me as he talked to my Mother about France, and my Dad, whom I knew was very brave. As he was putting on his hat to go, he said,

"Sorry, I forgot, I have something else for you,"

he laid three one pound notes on the table then he bent down and kissed my sister and me saying,

"That's from your Dad".

As he hurried down the yard, my Mother picked up the three pounds and said

"Get your coats on, we're going shopping!" And we did. Mum bought all the things that Christmas deserves, a large piece of beef from the market, fruit, nuts, a doll for my sister and a pop gun for me.

That Christmas of sixty two years ago will always live in my memory. That dear soldier, who was later killed, was the alchemist who transmuted an otherwise bleak, Christmas into gold. Dad was safe, the wonderful visitor had assured us. We even gave a penny to some carol singers. A memory to be treasured.

W.S.E.

After losing my father at the age of seven, we had to move from Canning Town to Stratford in the East End of London, to live near my Grandparents, who by the way loved us all dearly. Well, as it was nearly Christmas this was a solution of all our troubles at the time. Having packed our frugal belongings, we arrived three days before Christmas Eve. My Mother, being in a poor state of health, couldn't cope much, so we all went over Gran's. We helped her stir the pudding, everyone having a wish as well as a stir, and the lucky one scraping out the bowl. All our mouths were watering, and then, the smell of the cooking! We couldn't wait to get home and hang our socks up. They were thick black woollen ones at that, but with what excitement and anticipation we went to sleep and dreamt of what we might get - well, we could dream couldn't we?

The next morning we were up at the crack of dawn. What did we get? Well, I'll tell you. There was a lump of coal for luck, a brand new golden penny, a bag of home made sweets, also a whole orange and apple. We had never had a whole one before, what luxury! Dear old Gran had bought us all a small new toy, oh and also a few nuts. What a feast we had! My toy was a second hand doll all dressed up beautifully. What love lay behind my old gran's gifts, also the love of my dear mother, and all her efforts to make it a happy time!

Well, to crown it all, off we went to Christmas dinner over at Gran's. It was roast pork and all the trimmings. Also Grandad poured brandy, his own little gift, over the pudding and set it alight. What wonderful things families were those days, loyal and true! Apart from the dinner, Gran invited all the relations. Us children had to sit on the bed to make room for the others. Out came a barrel of beer for the grown ups, placed on a dresser. There was pop for us, plates of cut-up apples and oranges, also chestnuts and sweets, and mistletoe tied to the ceiling. The smell of the chestnuts roasting under a real, coal fire I shall never forget.

At midnight all the families went to go home, and, as we got to the door, it snowed heavily, making everywhere glisten and glow like a lot of decorated Christmas trees. We all knelt down in the snow and thanked God for a wonderful Christmas, and for our Mum, and our Gran. We have had wonderful times since, but none as memorial as that one with Mum, and all our families united, like real families should be.

L.E.

For me, Christmas really started when my Nanny told me that the time had come for the annual stir of the Christmas Pudding. This was quite a ceremony, I don't know what happened in other families for I was never with any other than my own family at Christmas, but in ours the stirring of the Pudding, together with the tense wishing that went with it, was something shared by all. On the great day my Mother and Father led the procession to the kitchen, Nanny and I followed (I was only a child) then came Jones the Butler, Jack and Osbert the two footmen, Mother's personal maid, Jessie, with the two housemaids bringing up the end.

As we entered the cavernous kitchen we were met by a smiling Mrs. French, the Cook, whose round, jolly looking face, shone like a great moon from the heat and from her exertions. She was flanked by Jenny the kitchen maid, and Mary the scullery maid, both of them with their arms bared to the elbows and their hands red and raw looking. We were all lined up, everyone very serious, and waited our turn to stir. The pudding occupied an enormous earthenware bowl and, as you stirred it, the most delicious smells rose from it, smells of spice and fruit and rich old ale. I found it very hard to stir, and was glad of a little help that Nanny gave me. It was so exciting and so hard not to let slip what you were going to wish, for if you did your wish would not come true. For some reason that I did not know the outside Staff never came to the stirring.

After this things to do with Christmas kept happening with ever increasing frequency, large and mysterious parcels and hampers were delivered by the local carrier's horse and cart, and more and more things had to be done. The village, of which my Father was the Squire, was quite small. There were thirty cottages scattered about the Parish, with a few larger houses for such as the Doctor and the Author. There were several farms, and, of course, the Vicarage.

For Christmas, Mother made up gift parcels for the poor of the village. This seemed to include most of them. About a week before the great day, Mother, Nanny and I started to get them ready. We included an ounce of tobacco, a large pork pie for families, jars of ginger and crystallised fruit, sometimes a chicken or perhaps a tin of ham, packets of tea and of course plenty of bags of sweets for the children. Mother consulted her list and called out what she wanted, then Nanny and I found it, and when it was all present and checked, it was done up in gay parcels and labelled.

On the morning of the day before Christmas, Mother ordered the big car, an enormous De Dion Bouton built like a stage coach, It was loaded up with all the parcels, and Mother and I set off. Albert the chauffer, dressed up in his smart brown uniform with gold braid on his peaked cap, drove us sedately down the long avenue of ancient chestnuts, out through the big gates, and down to the village. As each parcel was delivered there were bobbing curtseys, much flurry and fluster, and the old men, caps in hand, touching a respectful forelock, with a,

"Thankee Marm and young Marster, and a very happy Christmas to you all ".

Albert sat like a graven image, and the car seemed to glide from one cottage to the next as if drawn by some ethereal and invisible force.

In the evening there were the Carol Singers, the Church Choir. They gathered in a circle round a lantern hung from a pole, just outside the front door. I was allowed to stay up and watch and listen from the window of the best bedroom above the Hall. They sang all the old favourites, and sang them well. The trebles wavered a little now and then, but were soon held to the line by the rich, deep basses, and the strong voices of the tenors. They all came in after their singing, and Father thanked them. Mince pies, and something to warm them soon appeared. Then off I went to bed, knowing that I should never sleep, but always doing so within a few minutes.

What excitement in the morning. After a hasty breakfast, we all gathered in the Hall where presents for all were stacked round the huge Christmas tree that Blake, the Head Gardener, and two of his underlings had brought in a few days before, and which Nanny, helped by everyone, had decorated so beautifully. We always had lots of people staying for Christmas, Aunts, Uncles, old friends and sometimes new ones. There was such a buzz of delight and a crackling of papers, as everyone undid their presents, and read the good wishes on each parcel.

Then, on with our coats and hats, and a walk across the Park to Church. Sometimes, when it had snowed, the men pulled the ladies on little sledges. I can still hear the crunch and squeak of the snow under the runners, and the gay shouts and laughter of us all. Carols and prayers,and a few cheerful words for a sermon, a "Happy Christmas" all round, and then an invite to the Vicarage for a glass of sherry, and for me a little ginger wine.

Christmas dinner always took my breath away. The great table was a-glitter with the silver and the glass. The sideboard was piled high with endless good things, cold pheasant, partridge, great joints of ham, glistening tongues, pastries and preserves, great dishes of trifles, ice cream, fruit in abundance - my mouth ran water just to look at it all.

Then when we were all gathered and properly prepared came the great moment,

Jones, our Butler, flanked by the two footmen, entered bearing aloft a giant silver platter and on it, golden brown with wisps of steam rising, was the biggest turkey in the world, or so it seemed. Following the bird came Cook and her helpers and they got a great round of applause from us all. Father carved the first ceremonial slice from the majestic bird, Jones and his men piled the plates with practised speed, and we were soon busy eating. I was allowed to leave the table when I had finished, to go and play with my new toys whilst the grown ups sat on, cracking nuts and drinking their wine. Soon the ladies rested and the gentlemen adjourned to the smoking room where, wreathed in the fragrant aromas of fine cigars, they talked their men's talk and put the whole world to rights, or more likely dozed until the time for afternoon tea.

In the evening it was the turn of the staff to have their Christmas dinner. They had just the same as we did, and my Father and Mother and Aunts and Uncles made it their duty to serve and wait upon them. I too was expected to do my bit. The wine flowed, the good food was there a plenty, and soon the tongues loosened, and you have never in all your life heard such a joyful chattering and laughter as came from that kitchen so many years ago.

And it has passed away, and perhaps you will say "It sounds like a dream" and you would be right, it was a dream, a boy's dream. His mother was a widow. She took in washing to earn a meagre living. The home was one room up and one down. Outside, there was a wash house, and next to it a lavatory with its bucket. If we were lucky, there would be rabbit pie and dumplings for our Christmas dinner. With plum pudding after (boiled in the wash house copper after the clothes were up).

A dream, but what a lovely dream.

C.H.S.

Childhood memories are hazy, but those of early teenage are clearcut in my mind. From the age of thirteen I had been considered man enough to help on the farm during the holidays. When, therefore, George the horseman and Fred the stockman had a couple of days off at Christmas, Father and I rose early to do their work.

My job was to feed the horses. These intelligent, gentle giants would greet me with a whinny and move aside to let me empty a sieve full of oats and chaff into the manger, and fill the rack with hay. The bullocks, horned, clumsy and aggressive were fed by Father who emptied a mixture of chaff, mangolds and linseed cake from wicker skeps into their mangers, with the accompaniment of much shouting and waving of arms to keep the animals at bay.

After this, what an appetite we had for breakfast! And how we enjoyed opening presents when the table had been cleared! Then Mother would say,

"I can't cook dinner with a lot of useless people under my feet!"

So out we went for a walk across the fields, or into the village to exchange greetings with friends.

At midday we returned to do full justice to the meal of roast chicken or pheasant, sausages and vegetables galore, plum pudding (every helping held a sixpence!) followed by aptly named tipsy cake if appetite allowed. Late in the afternoon, the animals were fed again and bedded down, tea taken, and the family settled down to an evening of the usual party games.

Happy Christmas! Yet it was Boxing Day I most enjoyed. Early in the morning, we could hear George and Fred feeding the animals despite the fact that they were supposed to be on holiday. This was their unspoken way of accepting an invitation, also unspoken, to join in the traditional sport of the day - rabbiting. By nine o'clock they would be ready with ferrets, nets and spades, waiting for the assorted relatives and friends who also turned up for the event.

On cold days the rabbits bolted well, but on windy, damper ones they stayed underground. This meant that they had to be dug out laboriously following a line attached to a ferret. It was now that father did his party piece, saving us much time and energy. He would cut a long briar from the hedge and poke it down the hole until it met with some resistance. Pulling it out, he would point to some fur on the end of it. He would then lay his home-made detector on the ground above the run, and say knowingly,

"Dig below that fur and you'll find the rabbit." And we did.

George would return to the farmhouse just before lunch to collect a hamper filled with hot pasties and sausage rolls, bread and cheese, apples and flasks of coffee. How I enjoyed these open air meals, listening to their stories of past sporting exploits. The afternoon passed quickly. The bag was counted, and in the evening we played cards or party games again.

Now I spend my Happy Christmases watching my grandchildren following the same old country traditions.

C.L.M.

Wednesday 23rd December 1931, the eve of Christmas Eve. My head full of first love and family reunion. The close relatives who had moved away were coming for the holiday. The boy I had met at their home the previous Christmas was coming with them. Bubbling and a-tremble, here I was dragooned under Dad's instruction cleaning a rabbit and putting the eventual segments of pink carcase to steep overnight. Dad had been a cook once, a long time ago. Then we started the flaky pastry, salted flour and chopped up fat, left in the cloth-covered basin to settle ready for rolling out next day. Dad had a day off saved from his holiday.

A great cleaning of dried fruit followed - raisins to be stoned and chopped, peel to be neatly sliced and cross-sliced to give even, delicious fragments, a taste each of the lovely sugar out of the citron, hard and crunchy, lemon squeezed, nutmeg grated, mixed spice in. No popping to the shop for a jar of mince in those days! Good hard beef suet chopped and chopped to fine breadcrumb consistency, and another basin set aside for the big bake-up. Kitchen cleared up and flowers to arrange - I had a way with flowers even then. Hair washed and off to bed.

Next morning the house was astir early. The range fire had kept in, a a good raking and a little help set it blazing under the kettle.

"Come on mate," said Dad, "Get the rabbit on, I want the pie in and cooked and the mince pies done before dinner if we can."

There was some pressure in the kitchen. I was rolling pastry while Mother cooked bacon (small back), fried bread and yesterday's cold potato until it was browned and crispy. The rabbit simmered while we breakfasted. A final rolling of pastry, before it was divided for pie and mince, divided again for top and lining.The dish was lined, warm succulent white pieces forked in, a pouring of thick savoury gravy, and then the top crust put on, balanced over the china support in the middle. A hole was made to let the steam out. Dad cut out pastry leaves, brushed it all over with beaten egg. Then it was into the oven and a great sigh of relief.

Mother started on our vegetables for the next three days, while I rolled on making mince pies.

"Not too much, they'll boil over. That's right, damp the edges to seal them, now a hole in the top.." Dad was an exacting foreman. Sister Tilly was house cleaning as though it needed it which it didn't, and little brother Bert running errands.

The mid-day dinner was adequate but unexciting - that would come with the roast chicken tomorrow. We rested a little from the long battle with the range fire and the oven. Even

Dad was satisfied with the rabbit pie, Mother pleased with the mincemeat, a shade too much lemon, perhaps, but good. There was a confection called 'moonshine' to make for tomorrow's tea, extra jellies and blancmange, nuts to put out and bon-bons to get down from the top of the wardrobe in Mother's room (with instructions not to touch the other parcels).

I was cutting bread and butter for tea when I heard the quick footsteps pass the side of the bungalow. There was a sharp knock. Tilly opened the door, and Ted stood there! Six feet of eager youth, fit and glowing from the long walk down the lane, Boys Brigade badge on his lapel and a bulging travelling bag in his hands. I was, for once, speechless with delight.

Over tea he explained that he had the afternoon off, and couldn't wait to come down with the others on the evening train. They came in due time - Auntie laughing eyed and fluffy haired, Uncle large and hearty, Gladys uncomfortably taking after her father in size and her mother in exuberance, Win a bit overshadowed, carroty of hair and freckled. It was a hazy, crazy evening. Tilly and Auntie scooted off to the top of the lane to catch a bus to Southend to buy ham at Byatt's, cut paper thin and mouth-watering. Ten miles to get ham! They looked at the shops, along the High Street, right down to Brightwells, all still open at eight o'clock at night on Christmas

Eve. Dad was making icing-sugar flowers for the Christmas cake, shaping each petal with his thumb in the palm of his hand.

We were crowded that night, two families, plus, in a one-family dwelling. We girls slept in a made-up bed on the attic room floor. Ted slapt on the couch. All giggles subsided at last, and we slept.

It was a happy Christmas, until the Boxing night supper was laid with cheese and pickles and cold beef. Uncle took a look and joked,

"Coo,is this all you've got?"

Mother flushed and gasped. Dad looked up,

"No! Where's the rabbit pie?"

"We can't have that, it's cold," said Mother.

"It'll be alright cold," said Dad. And by jingo! it was. Flaky pastry two inches deep, meat in solid savoury jelly, easy to cut into slices. Pickles and pie - perfection!

For me, it rounded off the happiest Christmas ever.

E.N.

Chapter VIII
"Good night and God bless . . . "

"Just a song at twilight when the lights are low
And the flickering shadows softly come
and go.."

As I close my eyes to shut out the world, I can see in my mind's eye, my pretty dark-haired mother seated in a low chair in our small thatched cottage, her grey eyes alight with love, singing the popular songs of the day before we five girls scampered up the wooden staircase to bed.

"Come on now," she would say, before bed on school nights, "Just a lick and a promise."

The lick was cleaning round ears, necks and grubby grazed knees with a piece of flannel, whereas the promise was the Saturday night drubbing down, including a hair wash, in the old tin bath in front of the living room fire.

After tea had been cleared away and the washing up done, this bath would be taken down from its nail on the side of the shed next to the privy. Large black iron kettles already singing and spitting on the hob of the open fire, would be lifted off with a woollen kettle holder knitted by sister Phyllis (the only one of us who had mastered the art) and their contents poured in the bath. "Swish, swish" went Mother's hand mixing in cold water from a big enamel jug until the temperature was just right.

"Who's first?"

Each of us would try to scramble in, but we were always beaten by Mary,

"I'm the eldest," she would say, "So in I go before anyone pees in it," (which, of course, we all did, including Mary.)

After everyone had been dried and powdered with Robin starch, we were enveloped in long, white cotton nightgowns, already warmed over the tall, brass fire guard. Now it was time for our weekly dose of opening medicine, syrup of figs, which we all loved. Sometimes, however, Mother took a different bottle down from the mantle shelf.

"It will have to be this tonight," she would say, as one by one our noses were nipped and a teaspoonful of awful slimy castor oil was poured down our throats. Mother had some boiled sweets hidden away to reward us in these emergencies, but even today, although castor oil is tastless, I can never pluck up enough courage to swallow it.

Now the bath was pushed out of the way, Mother's chair brought forward, and we five fair-haired, blue-eyed little girls would forget our squabbles, and cluster round her knee for the treat of the evening. While the soft glow from the oil lamp, and the flames from the log fire sent shafts of flickering shadows up and down the walls, Mother's sweet voice would echo round the room singing 'Pack up your troubles' or 'Its a long long trail awinding' and other favourites of the day.

Then it was time for our nightly prayers, "Gentle Jesus, meek and mild", followed by a request to please take care of Father who was away fighting the Germans.

We raced up the stairs to see who could get into bed first. The two youngest made for mother's room at the front of the cottage, while we three argued over whose turn it was to sleep in the middle of our big double bed. A favourite game was "Guess what I'm drawing on your back?" and , needless to say, the one in the middle had the most pictures drawn on her. Eventually hands would fall limp, and the last sound we heard would be the wind in the boughs of our tall poplar tree.

D.W.

Bedtime was a very bleak occasion when I was a child. I was raised a convent, and we slept in dormitories with about sixty beds in each. The only heating was a large pipe running round the sides of the dormitory, and it didn't really heat the place very well. Our beds were iron-framed. On them we had a horse-hair palliasse, and a mattress filled with some sort of lumpy material. When we were old enough we had to put these lumps through a machine which chewed them up into more manageable pieces.

Our nightdresses were made of unbleached calico, so were our sheets. We had two grey blankets and a very hard pillow. The nightgowns were like large tents. That was just as well, as we had to undress and dress underneath them. It was considered very unlady-like and immodest to show one's body. In fact all these years later, I always dress and undress in a small room on my own.

At the two ends of the dormitory were large wooden stands with holes in which to place our wash basins. There were two taps in the middle, from which we fetched our water, and a gully to slop it away after washing. We had to slip our arms out of our nightdresses and tie the sleeves almost under our necks, so nobody could see below our shoulders.

Friday night was the worst night. We had to stand at our wash basins, so that the nun in charge could fill our tooth-mugs with Senna tea. She made sure that we had drunk every drop before we rinsed out our mugs. We only had two toilets, so you can imagine the stampede!

In bed we had to lie on our backs with our arms across our chests, over the covers. This was very cold in the winter. As soon as I thought our watch-dog was asleep, I used to roll on my side and tuck my legs up with my nightdress wrapped round them.

We never had a hot or cold drink after 4.30 p.m. tea time, and when I think of my own children's bedtime, and now my grand-children's and great grand-children's, it seems as if I was living in a scene from one of Dicken's novels. Anyhow we survived, and I suppose it toughened us to face the outside world.

B.P.

In 1917 electricity had not come to our little town in out of the way Cumberland, nor did it do so for several years after. (When it did, it was generated by the local iron works.) Until then almost all homes depended on gas for lighting: coal, coke and wood for fires; coal and gas for cooking.

In our house, nearly all the rooms were supplied with gas, no less than three having the brilliance of gas mantles. Above the corner shop, the big front room, cum-sitting room, cum-library, where my parents enjoyed a large well-sprung bed, sported no less than two mantled gas lights on splendid, elaborate, hinged brass wall-brackets.

My big sister's room had gas too, though with nothing more than a fantail jet; while we boys, poor things, had no gas at all.

My brother was seven years older than I was and my sister a year older than that. Consequently in that household I took the lowest rank, a mere child. Granted I was only seven, so perhaps it was to be expected that I should have to suffer what I felt to be the indignity, of getting sent to bed two hours before anybody else. To me it seemed cruel, shabby and distressing for a fine big chap.

There were two aspects that I particularly detested, being shut out from all the exciting family gossip round the table (which in a town full of aunts, uncles and cousins could be intensely interesting) and, if I am truthful, being made to suffer the nervousness of tackling the stairs alone in the dark.

I had a candle of course. There was one kept specially in a cupboard under the kitchen sink for my nightly use, together with a box of matches. Webster's matches I think they were. They carried a note about a Mr. Webster being the first to swim the English Channel. Can they still be bought, I wonder? I was sure that Mr Webster would not have been made to go to bed before any of the others in his home.

Yet every evening I was told to fetch my candle, and bring it into the living room before going to bed. I would delay the lighting as much as possible, still avidly listening so as to pick up as much of the conversation as I could, until firmly ordered to be off.

Now to open the door to those stairs, and reluctantly shut it after me. I was alone, with darkness all about me, closing in upon me, and my glimmer of light, waiting, perhaps, either to grab it from me, or to summon a sudden draught and extinguish it.

Even then I would have lingered and listened to the conversation through the door. But every step on the ancient stair creaked so loudly, that I had to keep on climbing them or the family would call out to know what was keepng me. I would hate them to know that I was nervous.

Once safe in my bedroom however, the tension subsided. It was not in fear, but in eager anticipation of something the others did not know about. Speedily I removed boots (sometimes it was clogs), long stockings with garters below the knees, and finally shorts. No vest or underpants, for these I did not wear. Not the shirt either, for I slept in that.

The something they did not know about, was a favourite pastime of mine, a fascinating little game I used to play nightly before hopping into bed. I played with fire.

My room, or rather our room, for my brother shared it, was about twelve foot by eight, having a sash window, better than most for it actually opened. (My father was something of a health fanatic). It had lino on the floor and a small carpet by the bed. The rest of the furniture was simple enough. It consisted of a four foot bed with a firm straw mattress and an enamel chamberpot underneath (the W.C. being out-doors). There was a canary wood dressing table, without jug or basin as we all washed in turn at the kitchen sink, and a small dark set of book-shelves well filled. There was a bentwood chair matching those in the shop downstairs, and an eighteen inch square, bamboo table by the bed. It was on this table, of of course, that I placed the candlestick. Then began all the fun.

There was always at least one burnt-out matchstick in the surround, and a pretty pool of pearly wax about the burning wick. Dip the matchstick in the pool, and it eagerly drank up a portion of the wax. Now touch the flame and, hey presto, the light in the room was at least twice as good. Before the flame crept too near my dear, young fingers, I carefully put it down in the bottom of the candlestick where I could enjoy watching it burn away merrily. And how attractive it appeared to me then! I would be horrified if I saw a child doing it today. When it had exhausted the wax it had soaked up I simply applied more, peeling the wax off with my fingernail which had run down the side of the candle.

Of course, this secondary flame needed constant attention, but that was all part of the fascination. I learned to add just enough wax to keep the carbon skeleton of a match alight, yet not too much as to allow the conflagration to grow too large.

Beside the harvesting of wax from the candle to fuel the charred fragment, and prodding the latter so that it could always get just the amount required, it was necessary periodically to check the temperature of the candlestick lest it scorch the table top. I must always remember that the heat would be steadily accumulating and very gradually spreading. The time inevitably came when action must be taken.

My plans were ready. I simply dived across the room for my beloved copy of "Alice in Wonderland". Lifting the hot candlestick, I placed the book under one side, the box of matches under the other, and balanced the fiery furnace upon them.

The game could now continue for quite a long time. So long as there was plenty of space for the heat to escape, the book well away from the hottest part, and the matchbox in contact only along its least explosive end and not too far under, all was well.

Loss of sleep never seemed to trouble me. But sooner or later I would hear my mother and sister move away from the supper table and towards the kitchen to wash up, and my brother to get firewood for the morning. This was the signal for me to extinguish my miniature bonfire, scatter the remains, and hop into bed. There I would blow out the candle, and wait in the darkness for the contraption to cool. Several minutes later, I would hear my brother putting a foot on those creaky stairs.

Now it remained only to reach out in the darkness, remove the book and matchbox from under the candlestick, turn over against the wall, and pretend I was sleeping. Such was the advantage of being a pure innocent child, in two minutes I really was . . . asleep.

E.H.

Chapter IX

"The good old days . . . "

I suppose I am like a swan, with my head turned back under my wing seeking protection from what will come. Looking back, what changes have passed me by! What to come?

Born into a world of war, followed by hard depressing years, then more years of war, which boomed into years of luxury living. Now again back to soaring prices and unemployment. One fears to look ahead.

I remember those bad houses where people slept three and four to a bed. There were no baths and no hot water. Now, how lovely it is to turn on the switch, a room full of light, a steaming bath.

"Oh, you must put in the fairy liquid, or the bath salts, according to what you are washing."

Bye roads were mud and water tracks. I trudged,very young, on early mornings to fetch the milk. I was shouted at by the farmer's wife,

"You are late, girl! There's no skimmed left now. It's after six o'clock."

Today it greets me in a lovely bottle when I get up.

The roads now are a network of jigsaw turnings, under and over, filled with smelling, four-wheeled vehicles. No more hanging on the back of carts, with the driver swishing his whip round to get you off. The smell was there then, worse. Horse dropping fouled everywhere, and people emptied their dirty water in the gutter.

Fried plaice, steak and mushrooms, chops, prawn cocktails, peaches and cream, slimming bread and salad are our meals now. How I remember the smell of those meat puddings, shin pies, Irish stews, really thick soups, new-baked bread and fruitcake, with Grandma's homemade beer for elevenses. I remember those bloaters cooked on the toasting fork in front of the fire.

Then there was Christmas, when the whole family gathered. Everyone did their party piece, and Christmas was every night from Christmas Eve till New Year's Day and 'first footers'. How we used to laugh then! Now it's somewhere to eat Christmas day and the television.

Those long drab skirts my mother wore when I was a child - I thought she was sixty. Then came the short hair and light and gay dresses, now we return to the long skirts again and long hair, - life's ever changing. Gone are the shops where you sat on chairs to be served, and half the shop was brought for you to view, and money clanged in little boxes on wires across the ceiling, returning you the change.

When you were sick, it was rather nice. You had different things to eat from the rest of the family. Everyone fussed round you. But it's not like that any more - a box of pills, a bottle of lemonade, and you are on your feet.

Changes change us all - like the new buildings. We see tall masses of buildings. We see tall masses of concrete and glass, solid, hard. Some I like, some I don't, That's life I suppose.

The greatest changes I see are in people. Neighbours were in every sense neighbours - a bit nosey, sometimes, perhaps, but always there to laugh or cry in sunshine or in sorrow. They were friends indeed.

M.L.S.

The beautiful blossoms adorning the trees in my village this Spring, recalled a flood of memories of my childhood in our London back garden, and of the huge cherry tree that dominated it.

There was no T.V. in those days to keep my sisters, brother and I cooped up indoors, neither did we have the sophisticated toys of today, but we had something more precious to us than television or toys, our cherry tree. A tree so enormous that the spread of its branches covered more than half of our garden.

In Spring, it was bedecked with radiant white blossom, it was a vision of beauty for us, and for everyone living down our road. It towered higher than the house and dwarfed every other tree.

In Summer, the sweet White Heart cherries hung delectably among the soft green leaves, waiting for us to pick them, and to drape them in pairs over our ears like ear-rings, before we ate them.

When Autumn turned the leaves to gold and bronze, and the gusty winds flung them to the ground, we crunched them happily beneath our feet.

Winter changed the bare branches and twigs into black lace against a pale blue sky. Then, wrapped in warm clothes, we ran round the garden playing "He" and "Off ground touch".

My Father had planted the cherry tree when he was a small boy. He had moved from Scotland to London with his family, and a friend had given him the little tree to plant in the garden of his new home. It had grown through the years of my Father's youth, and now it was our haven, sheltering us from the spring showers and the hot summer sun.

It was our plaything. We climbed it. We swung on it. We hung downwards from it. We even built a ricketty tree house in it. The tree house only supported two of us at a time, but how we gloried in it, and looked down at inferior, treeless gardens, while we munched ginger biscuits and chewed the colourless gum that oozed from the cracks in the bark.

Our three cousins who lived next door, enjoyed the tree as much as we did. Together we played wonderful games. Our dog, Bob, also one of the family, joined in whenever he could. He was only a rough-haired, black and white mongrel terrier, but we loved him dearly, and he gave us his complete devotion.

We used to hurry home on summer days to have tea in the garden under the tree. Our tea tasted like nectar to us, or it would have done had we known what nectar was. The tiny green caterpillars that descended on silken threads above our plates did nothing to detract from our healthy appetites. On summer evenings, gnats would dance in little groups under the tree, and we would clap our hands together to see how many we could squash at a blow (ugh!).

My birthday in June was celebrated each year with a garden party. My Mother threaded coloured glass lanterns containing night lights through the branches. When they were alight, it looked like fairyland to us.

On Saturday afternoons we went to the local flea-pit where, for the price of two and a half old pennies, we saw our favourite film stars of the silent screen. Later, we re-enacted the films in our garden. A cushion on a low branch of the tree made an excellent steed for a Cowboy or Indian. When we followed a Tarzan serial, our tree became a jungle. We would hang out from the branches screaming "CATS" to Bob. This sent him into a frenzy of excitement, barking and leaping madly into the air. To us he was a raging lion, leopard or ferocious grizzly bear.

The hullabaloo brought Mother running onto the scene. She would drag poor protesting Bob back to the house where he would continue to whine and scratch the back door, believing we might all be in some terrible danger.

Bob had come to us when he was a cuddly puppy of six weeks old, and he shared our lives for twelve years. He was just a grand companion and an excellent watch dog. Every morning before breakfast we would let him out for a run. After about fifteen minutes he would announce his return by hurling himself at the front door. He would then be let in for his dish of tea.

He fell asleep for the last time on a grey autumn day. The rain dripping mournfully from the tree outside seemed to mirror the tears within the house.

We were sitting in the front room, about three weeks later, when there was a terrific crash against the front door. We all looked up, startled, at the familiar sound. My little sister shouted,

"It's Bob!" She burst into tears as she remembered. I was sitting in the window seat and could see the front door clearly. There was no one there, no one in the front garden, no one at all in the road. Was it Bob? Bidding us a last goodbye?

When my Father died, my Mother sold the house, and that same year our cherry tree was struck by lightning. Half of it was killed and during the following year it was struck again. Our dear old cherry tree was gone for ever.

Both Bob and the cherry tree are gone, long since. We children have all grown up and scattered, but our London back garden, the magnificent cherry tree, and beloved Bob, will remain in our memories forever.

E.M.C.

How accurately can one remember all those years ago? Is it possible to recall the excitement felt by a little girl of ten going on an outing alone with Grandma and Grandpa? I was the eldest and our family always went about together, so that it was special to be going by myself, and being the first one to do so.

It was the year of the British Empire Exhibition at Wembley. Grandma and Grandpa had come to stay with us especially to visit the Exhibition. They had a son in Africa and we had relations in India. Something to be proud of and certainly not to be missed. They said they would take me on one occasion, then my sister on another.

When the day arrived, my head was awhirl with my mother's instructions to be good, to keep with Grandma and not to worry her by running off. I must remember that she could not keep up with my usual darting hither and thither, and above all I must not get lost. Children were always getting lost at Wembley, and I was to reassure my Grandparents that I was safe by being constantly at their side.

We caught the new Metropolitan line to Wembley Park, recently built for the Great Exhibition. I wonder what I was wearing at the time? In the mid-twenties waists were low. I remember that I had a dress with a straight bodice to below the waistline, then a skirt which ended just below the knee. It was dark red, and I felt very grown-up in it because it was similar to the dresses of the adults around me. I remember the tight little cloche hats and the floating diaphanous scarves.

Grandma and Grandpa always looked the same to me. They dressed as part of the older generation. I must be the same age now as they were then, but Grandma would never, never have worn trousers, or any colour other than black. Do my Grandchildren have difficulty in getting the generations straight in their minds because Granny drives a car, wears trousers and sits on the floor to play with them? I don't think so. One grandson calls me 'Ope' (OAP), even while expecting me to be as energetic as his mother.

Well, we arrived at Wembley Park Station, and the entire train load of passengers streamed along the road to the Exhibition, up the rise and through the gates, flanked by those twin towers which are still there today.

There was so much to see! All this was part of our great Empire, and we were the Mother Country. I remember the glorious Indian Pavilion and the lovely saris of the women. Was there a model of the Taj Mahal and were we told its story? I recall a feeling of sadness from this display.

The exhibit from this country was a coal mine. We went inside to see lifelike models of men at work. The impression of darkness, of everything black is with me still. I recall the men's faces in the twilight, streaked with black. I was glad to get out into the daylight again. I had a strange feeling of guilt that men lived like that while I was enjoying the sunshine.

But best of all, I remember the Funfair. I wonder what my Grandparents felt about it because I went on everything alone. I cannot imagine Daniel letting me do that today.

"Come with me!"

he would say, fully expecting my company in everything that we do. We do do it together, from pushing him in a swing to riding in a bumper car. But I went alone, climbing to the top of the big slide, the 'Jack and Jill'.

One went down its tower sitting on a mat. The speed increased quite dramatically as one set off. I could not have been sitting squarely on the mat. Knowing myself as a child, I am certain that I never asked how to sit or what to do. I would have been much too shy. So, off I went, and I was terrified!

What had looked such fun at the bottom of the slide, when I had watched the riders come down laughing, shouting and waving their arms, was not the same alone and askew. I bumped from side to side, and my right arm was grazed above and below the elbow with a searing hot pain. Poor Grandpa and Grandma that I should have seen the Indian Pavilion and the Coal Mine, and let it all pale into insignificance because I grazed my arm.

Nevertheless, I collected stamps for many years, and I always lingered over one page with two large square stamps, one red, one brown. They were the Wembley Exhibition stamps. Just looking at them reminds me of the crowds, the beauty, the pride, and the sight of quite other ways of life, that the Exhibition gave. Children today would not feel quite the same excitement at the strangeness of of it all. To a child of the mid-twenties, here was geography come alive. This was real. New Zealand butter came from an actual place, and oranges from Africa bore the imprint of black fingers. The world had been brought much closer to our lives and our imaginations.

C.M.G.

The good old days? Looking back over the past sixty or more years, I often wonder why those times were called 'good'. I suppose it is because the ordinary person's mind tends to forget the unpleasant things in life, seizes on a few crumbs of joy and, over the years makes them into something marvellous.

It is wonderful to look back on our Sunday afternoons and remember how the whole family gathered round the glowing fire, ears strained to catch the first tinkle of the muffin man's bell. Then to remember the excitement as the muffins were toasted on long forks at the fire. These, with winkles or shrimps, also bought at the door, and the cakes that mother had spent the morning baking, made our Sunday's high tea special.

Sunday tea was a ritual. No matter how poor the family, some sort of show had to be made for this particular meal. Uncles, Aunts, Grandparents came visiting, and with no television or wireless, the evening often developed into a sing song round the piano, and organised amusement for the children until it was time for bed.

In those days children were subjected to far stricter discipline than is usual now. I think many of the present 'older people' would agree that it was a 'good' thing. Children were not brought up to be little angels, far from it, but they were taught to observe a code of conduct, to make life more pleasant for all. Not only their parents, but other adults took an interest in putting them on the right path. A policeman seeing a child up to mischief, would clout the offender, either with his gloves or rolled up cape.

School was a place for the teaching of right and wrong - never take unfair advantage or hit below the belt. Even the comics and children's magasines stressed the importance of being fair, and 'playing the game'. There was no violence or vandalism, as we know it today: no wrecking of trains or telephone boxes. The robbing and beating up of old ladies was unheard of.

One often hears that youngsters are in trouble because they are deprived or come from a poor home. The youngsters of the 'good old days' were almost all deprived, yet they knew that it was wrong to wreck and rob. People seemed to have more inherent pride. The times were extremely hard, yet people would do anything rather than seek help from any charity.

We had great numbers of men protecting our huge Empire. Soldiers or sailors in their uniforms were a common sight in our streets. So, too, were children running about in all weather without boots and stockings, children in dirty ragged clothes, children who stood with their noses pressed to the panes of the baker's shop window or who hung about the factory gates, begging for the scraps left over from employee's mid-day meals.

We were of course, one of the richest countries in the world. Other old people, looking back, may agree that it was a pity that these riches could not have been more evenly distributed. Happiness then meant a job, any sort of job, as long as it brought in the money to buy bread and pay the rent. Young couples could rarely afford to put down the deposit to buy a houses. There was no Health Service or Welfare Service and the Old Age Pension was thirty seven and a half new pence per week. The great fear of old people was that they might finish up in the workhouse.

There was a kind of comradeship among people, when all were hard up to a greater or lesser degree. The fact of being "in the same boat" seemed to draw people together. There was very little "trying to keep up with the Joneses" - it just could not be done. The struggle was to keep warm, to be able to feed the children, and, joy of joys, perhaps to have a copper or two over at the end of the week, to pay for a pint or a visit to the pictures.

The 'good old days' are created by our memories and imaginations. The present time is really the good days, if only people can be made to realise it, and not blind themselves to the facts of how tough life can be.

G.F.S.

THE END